DREAMWEAVER ULTRADEV 4

for PC/MAC

DREAMWEAWER ULTRADEV 4

Copyright - Editions ENI - August 2001
ISBN: 2-7460-1368-1
Original edition: 2-7460-1284-7

ENI Publishing LTD

5 D Hillgate Place
18-20 Balham Hill
London SW12 9ER

Tel: 020 8673 3366
Fax: 020 8673 2277

e-mail: publishing@ediENI.com
http://www.eni-publishing.com

Studio Factory collection directed by Corinne HERVO
English edition by Andrew BLACKBURN

This book describes the Dreamweaver UltraDev 4 functions concerning the creation of dynamic web sites. It was designed to enable you to find which options to use or which action to perform to achieve the required result, as quickly and easily as possible. The screens illustrated throughout complement the explanations given, by showing the dialog box that corresponds to an action or by giving a precise example.

Each chapter relates to a specific topic: installing servers, defining the various database connection mechanisms (ASP, JSP, ColdFusion), managing record sets to search databases, structuring different types of query, creating results pages, using Live Data, managing site access permissions, creating master and detail pages, using dynamic objects, managing records, creating dynamic text and form fields, dynamic html attributes, using other data sources and Ultra-Dev extensions.

A useful list of server behaviors and live objects can be found in the appendix, along with a **glossary** of terms and the **index**.

Typographic conventions

To help you find the information you need quickly and easily, the following conventions have been adopted:

bold indicates the option to take in a menu or dialog box.

italics is used for introductory and explanatory comments.

Ctrl represents a key from the keyboard. When two keys appear side by side, they should be pressed simultaneously.

The following symbols indicate:

 the action to be carried out (such as activating a button or clicking with the mouse).

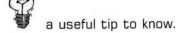 a general comment about the command in question.

a useful tip to know.

Introduction

Local Web server

UltraDev interface

Defining a site

Connecting to databases

Recordsets

Introducing SQL

Setting-up queries

Creating results pages

Testing your dynamic pages

Managing site access rights

Detail pages

Related pages

Live objects

Managing records

Dynamic forms and text

Dynamic HTML attributes

Other data sources

UltraDev extensions

Appendix

Presenting Dreamweaver UltraDev

Dreamweaver UltraDev for PC or Macintosh provides the full set of Dreamweaver page creation features along with specific tools for interacting with databases. These tools allow you to:

— query a database using a search form,

— create a navigation bar to browse the entries in a results page,

— manage identifiers and passwords for accessing certain pages of a Web site,

— update or delete information in a database,

— manage application variables, session variables and cookies.

You can develop dynamic Web applications using the following server technologies:

— ASP: Active Server Pages (Microsoft)

— JSP: Java Server Pages (Sun Microsystems)

— ColdFusion (Allaire Corporation)

UltraDev is an ASP, JSP or ColdFusion development environment. It generates the server-side scripts your application requires. To interact with a database, you must be able to implement a relational database and use the principal SQL (Structured Query Language) statements. Provided you master the associated page development technologies as well, you can also develop your own script libraries.

To test your dynamic pages, you need either to have access to a Web server or to install a local server on your computer. You must have the required configuration, according to your server technology, your operating system, your database and your Web server.

 With the Macintosh version of UltraDev, you need access to a remote server, as you cannot test your pages locally.

Static and dynamic Web sites

Introduction

Dynamic Web sites include e-commerce sites, online catalogues and customised press reviews. Most dynamic Web sites interact with databases. UltraDev allows you to display the results of a multi-condition search page, to authenticate your visitors, to customize a product offer according to the visitor's profile, to manage access to specific site pages, to update client profile information in a database and to monitor a browsing session (by tracing connection time and the nature of the pages visited).

The server computer runs ASP, JSP or ColdFusion scripts, creates the page contents dynamically and sends them to the client computer.

In the case of multi-condition search forms, the server-side ASP, JSP and ColdFusion scripts include all the necessary statements for database connection, data extraction and data formatting.

Dreamweaver UltraDev allows you to develop dynamic page content using the following technologies:

— ASP (Active Server Pages) from Microsoft,

— JSP (Java Server Pages) from Sun Microsystems,

— ColdFusion from Allaire.

For this purpose, you need an application server that can run the ASP, JSP and ColdFusion scripts that UltraDev generates.

Static sites

The client computer sends the Web server an http query, such as http://www.mysite.com/page.html, for example. The Web server finds the required page and returns it to the client computer.

Dynamic sites

A dynamic site combines HTML code with code specific to the technology used (ASP, JSP or ColdFusion server side scripts).

The client computer sends the Web server an http query, such as http://www.mysite.com/search.asp, http://www.mysite.com/search.jsp or http://www.mysite.com/search.cfm, for example.

The application server runs the ASP, JSP or ColdFusion scripts, creates the html page dynamically and returns it to the client computer.

The client browser receives a page whose source code contains only HTML items, with no programming lines. The original page on the server contains all the programming statement.

 Important note: a dynamic site is a site that interacts with a database. This term does not refer to any DHTML items or dynamic Flash animations that a site's pages may contain.

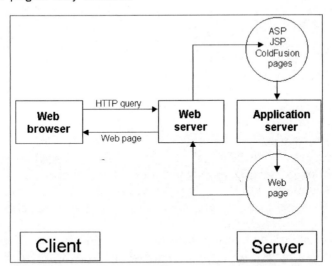

The above diagram shows dynamic page processing on the server.

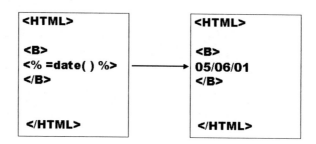

In the above example, the client computer requests a dynamic page. The <%_%> part of the script runs on the application server. The application server returns the result of this execution. The Web server replaces this part of the script with this value and returns the page to the client machine.

ASP, JSP and ColdFusion technologies

 Remember to check that your Web server is properly configured to run each of these technologies.

ASP: Active Server Pages

Microsoft's ASP (Active Server Pages) technology provides a set of server components incorporated into IIS (Internet Information Server) or PWS (Personal Web Server). You can use ASP without installing an application server, as the Web server performs this role.
Dreamweaver UltraDev allows you to develop with ASP version 2 using the VBScript or JavaScript programming languages.
ASP runs on Windows NT or Windows 2000 servers and on Windows 95/98 workstations (provided you have installed the Personal Web Server).
The Chilli!Soft engine allows you to run ASP on Linux or Solaris platforms.
ASP files have .asp name extensions and ASP scripts are delimited by `<% scripts %>` tags.

For example:

```
<%
dim name
name=Request.Form("name")
%>
```

JSP: Java Server Pages

Sun Microsystems developed JSP (Java Server Pages), which uses the Java programming language.
JSP runs on a large number of Web servers on Windows, Linux, Unix, Solaris and Macintosh.
JSP files have .jsp name extensions. JSP scripts are delimited by `<% scripts %>` tags.

For example:

```
<%
name=request.getParameter("name")
%>
```

ColdFusion

Allaire Corporation developed ColdFusion, as a proprietary technology. The ColdFusion server runs on Windows, Linux, and Solaris.
The ColdFusion programming language uses special tags called CFML tags.
ColdFusion files have .cfm or .cmfl name extensions and ColdFusion statements require specific CFML tags.
For example:

```
<CFOUTPUT>#form_inscription.name#</CFOUTPUT>
```

Introduction

To test the pages you create, you need a local or remote Web server and an application server that can run ASP, JSP or ColdFusion scripts.
This chapter will explain how you can install a Web server and ASP, JSP and ColdFusion application servers for testing your dynamic pages on Windows.

 If you are developing on Macintosh, you must have access to a remote server, as you cannot test your pages locally.

Web server for ASP, JSP and ColdFusion

You can install the Microsoft Personal Web Server version 4.0. This application runs with Windows 95, 98 and NT Workstation. In fact, Personal Web Server is a reduced version of IIS (Internet Information Server).

Windows 2000 provides a complete version of IIS 5.0.

The Windows 98 CD-ROM contains the Personal Web Server in a folder named Add-ons/PWS. Alternatively, you can download it from the Microsoft Web site.

 Important note: there is no server that allows you to test ASP and ColdFusion pages on Macintosh.

Microsoft does not recommend that you install the Personal Web Server on Windows Me (see the technical note Q266456 "Personal Web Server Is Not Included with Windows Millennium Edition" on the Microsoft Web site, at the address: **http://support.microsoft.com/support/kb/articles/ Q266/4/56.ASP**).

Downloading the Microsoft Personal Web Server

If you are using Windows 95/98 or Windows NT Workstation, you must download the Personal Web Server from the Microsoft Windows NT 4.0 Option Pack.

⊡ Connect to the following address:
http://www.microsoft.com/msdownload/ntoption/askwiz.asp

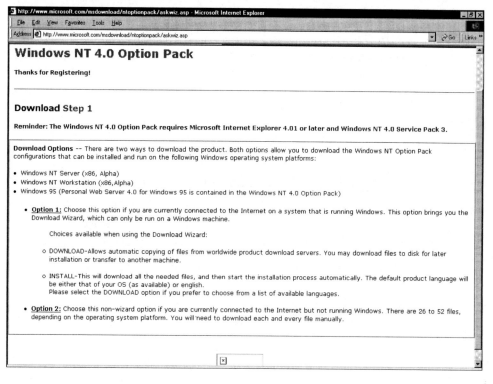

⊡ Click the **Option 1** link.

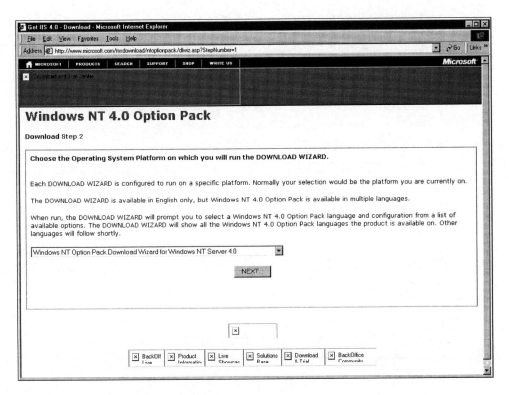

Select your operating system:

Click the **NEXT** button.

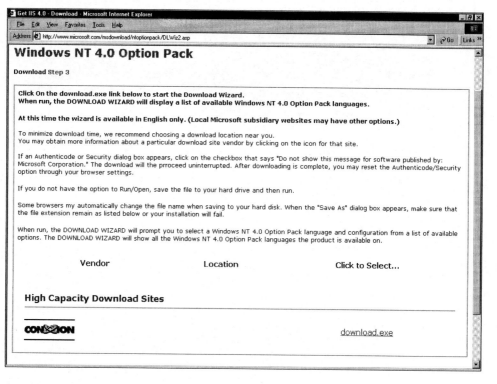

⊡ Click the **download.exe** link, choose to **Save this program to disk** and indicate the folder to which you want to download the file.

*The (520 KB) **download.exe** program allows you to install or download the Personal Web Server.*

⊡ In your **Windows Explorer**, double-click the **download.exe** file to download the Personal Web Server.

⊡ Click **Yes** to accept the **Licence Agreement**.

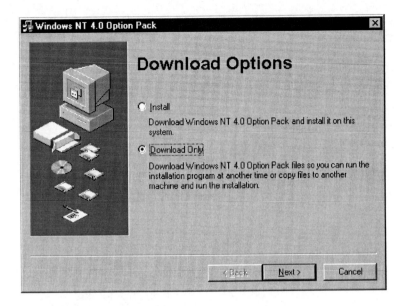

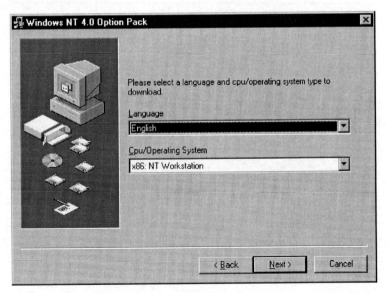

Choose the **Download Only** option to download the installation files.

Click the **Next** button.

⊡ If necessary, choose the **Language** you want to use and your **Cpu/Operating System**.

*For example, choose **English** and **x86: NT Workstation** to install the server in English on Windows NT Workstation.*

⊡ Click the **Next** button.

⊡ Choose the type of installation you want to make:

  — **Typical installation**: to install the basic components, by default,

  — **Minimal Installation**: to install the minimum features for deploying a Web site,

  — **Full Installation**: to install the full set of components.

⊡ Click the **Next** button.

⊡ Select the folder where you want to save your installation files.

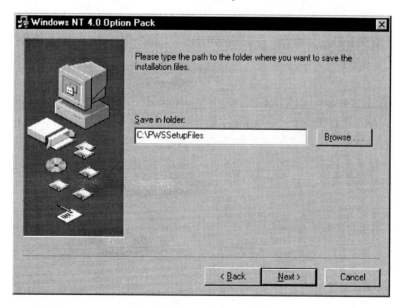

⊡ Click the **Next** button.

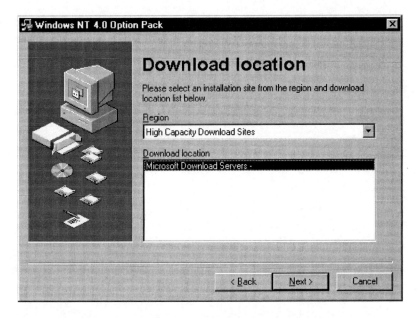

☐ Choose the site from which you want to download the files.

☐ Click the **Next** button.

The installation program starts downloading the Personal Web Server, version 4.0:

⊡ When the download is finished, you can install the Personal Web Server on your system (see **Installation procedure**, below).

Installation procedure

⊡ Open either the **Add-ons/Pws** folder on the Windows 98 CD-ROM or the folder in which you saved the installation files during the download procedure.

⊡ Run the **setup.exe** file.

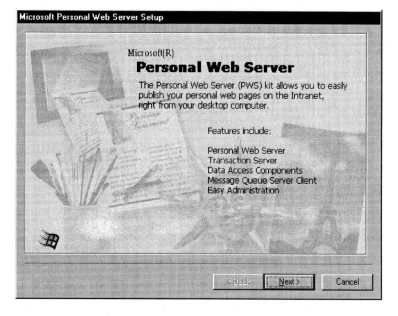

⊡ Click **Next**.

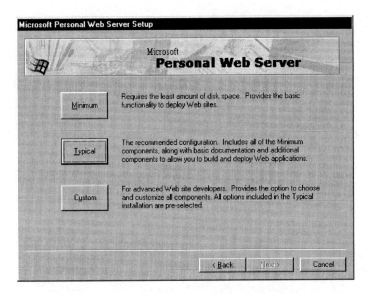

Choose the **Typical** installation.

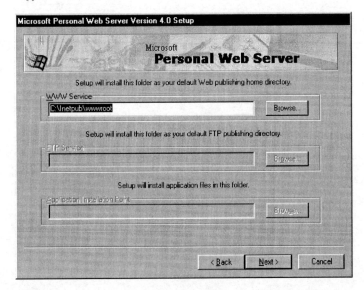

*The Web server root directory is **C:\inetpub\wwwroot**. This will be the home directory for all your sites.*

⊡ Click **Next** to complete the installation.

Once the installation is complete, you must restart your computer:

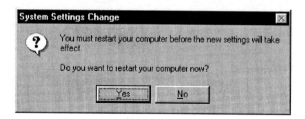

Starting the personal Web server

⊡ Click the **Start** button and select **Programs - Internet Explorer - Personal Web Server** (or select the program group in which you installed the server). Choose **Personal Web Manager**.

Alternatively, you can click the 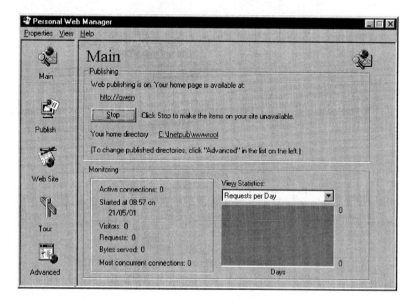 *icon on the right of the taskbar.*

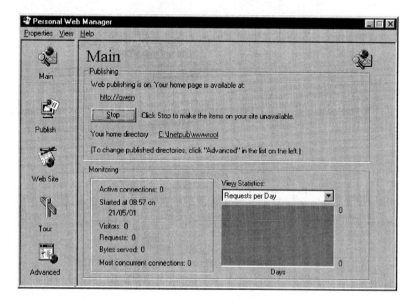

Your Web server is now running.

⊡ The **Stop** button allows you to stop the server (once you have stopped your server a **Start** button replaces the **Stop** button; click this button to re-start the server).

⊡ Note the **http** address of your computer: as the identifier of your machine, Windows uses the computer name defined on the **Identification** page of the **Control Panel-Network** dialog box.

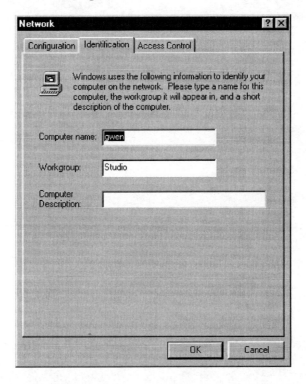

 Do not use spaces, dots, accentuated characters or other extended cha-racters in your **Computer Name**.

⊡ Start your Web browser and enter the **http** address of your computer in the **HTTP://computer name** format.

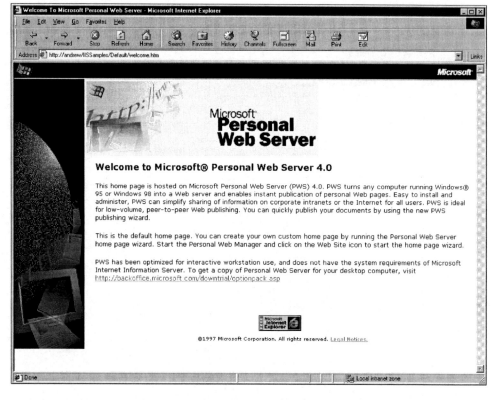

If you successfully installed your Web server, the default **Personal Web Server** *home page will appear.*

The Personal Web Server accepts one of the three following addresses:
- http://computer_name
- http://127.0.0.1 (the IP address of the local Web server)
- http://localhost (the alias of local Web server IP address).

ASP application server

The Internet Information Server or the Personal Web Server 4.0 automatically provides the ASP components. On the other hand, the Personal Web Server 2.0 did not include the ASP components: in this case you must install the Web server (pws.exe) followed by the ASP application (asp.exe).

ColdFusion application server

The Dreamweaver UltraDev CD-ROM provides a mono-user version of the ColdFusion server. Alternatively, you can download an evaluation copy of ColdFusion from the Allaire site at the address: http://www.alaire.com. When you run the ColdFusion Setup program, choose the **Personnal Web server** as the Web server.

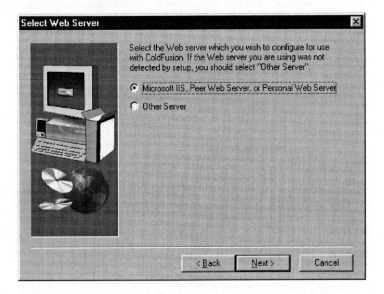

Installing a Web server for JSP

The Dreamweaver UltraDev CD-ROM provides a test version of the (Allaire) JRun server. However, you must install the Java Runtime Environment before you install Jrun (you can install the Java Runtime Environment directly from the jr30w application of the Dreamweaver UltraDev CD-ROM. Alternatively, you can download the Java Development Kit (JDK) from the Sun site at the address: http://java.sun.com /j2se/1.3).

As with the Java Runtime Environment, you can install the JRun server by double-clicking the **jr30w** application in the **JRun** folder of the Dreamweaver UltraDev CD-ROM. Select the **Allaire Jrun Server**.

Click **Next** and click **Yes** if you accept the license agreement.

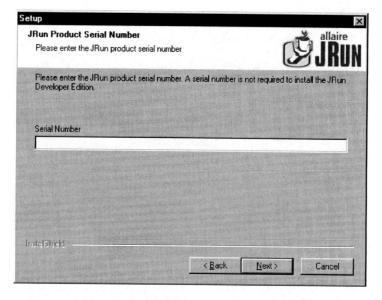

Click **Next** directly, as you do not need to enter a serial number to install the Jrun Developer Edition. Specify the JRun installation folder, as necessary and click **Next**.

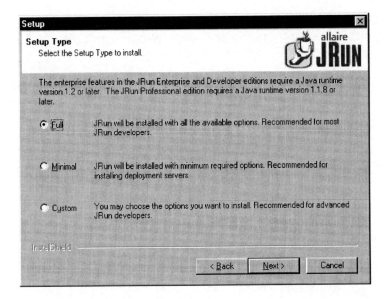

Choose the type of installation you require and click **Next**. Select the program folder and click **Next**.

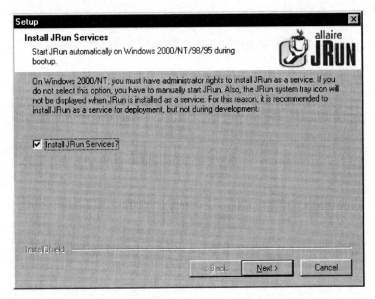

⤆ Choose to **Install JRun** services, and click **Next**. Select the Java runtime application you installed and click **Next**. Read the **JVM Advisor** notes and click **Next**.

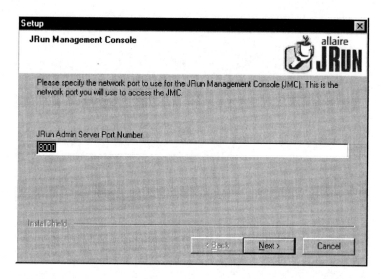

⤆ Enter a **Port Number** for your JRun Management Console and click **Next**.

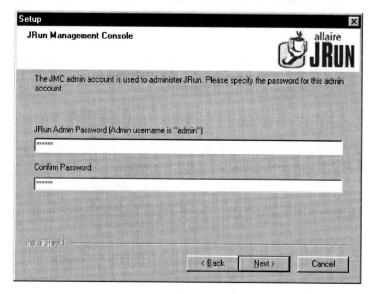

🔁 Enter a **Password** for the JRun administrator and click **Next**. Enter your contact details if you would like to receive JRun news.

🔁 Click **Next**.

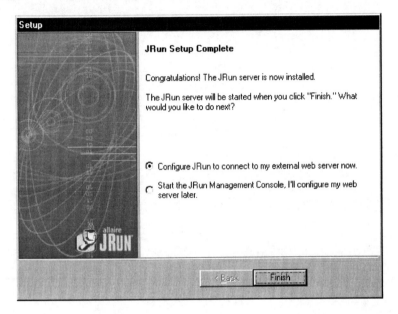

🔁 Click **Finish**.

JRun starts the Web server configuration procedure. This procedure comprises four steps.

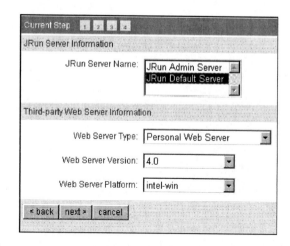

⊡ Under **JRun Server Information** choose the **JRun Default Server**.

⊡ Under **Third-party Web Server Information** choose:

— Web Server Type: **Personal Web Server**

— Web Server Version: **4.0**

— Web Server Version: **Intel-win** (for Windows installation).

⊡ Click **next**.

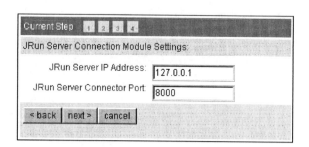

*JRun configures the Personal Web Server **IP Adress** and **Port**.*

⊡ Click **next**.

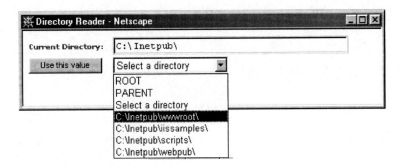

⊟ As the **Current Directory**, select the home directory that contains the personal Web server scripts.

⊟ Open the Select a directory pop-up menu and select the **C:\Inetpub\wwwroot** directory.

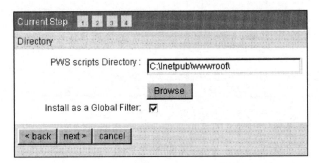

⊟ Click **next**.

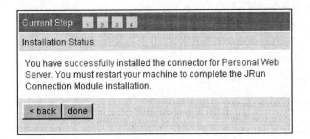

You have completed the installation of the JRun application server for the personal Web server.

⊡ Click **done** and restart your computer.

Managing your personal Web server

Starting and stopping your Web server

⊡ Click the **Start** button and select **Programs - Internet Explorer - Personal Web Server** (or select the program group in which you installed the server). Choose **Personal Web Manager**.

Alternatively, you can click the 🌀 *icon on the right of the taskbar.*

*By default, UltraDev selects the **Main** view: the **publishing** frame of the console shows the **http** address of your Web server.*

⊡ Click the **Stop** button to stop your Web server or click the **Start** button to start your Web server.

*The home directory is **C:\inetpub\wwwroot**.*

Changing the default home page

⊡ Click the **Advanced** button 🎵 in the views bar on the left of the **Personal Web Manager** console.

⊡ In the **Default Document(s)** box, enter the names of your default home pages. For example, index.html, index.asp (Microsoft uses the file names Default.htm, Default.asp).

Creating a virtual directory

A virtual directory is useful in two cases:

*- if the home directory of your Web site is not in the **C:\inetpub\wwwroot** folder,*

*- if you want to hide the name of the home directory in the **http** address of your site.*

The idea is to use the name of your virtual directory instead of the real name of your Web site's home directory. For example, you can use **http://localhost/Catalogue** *(alias) instead of* **http://localhost/Disksite**.

Click the **Advanced** button 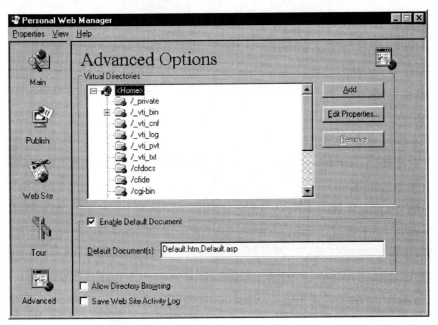.

UltraDev provides the list of **Virtual Directories** for your server. You can add or modify a virtual directory. To add a virtual directory:

Click the **Add** button.

In the **Add Directory** dialog box, click the **Browse** button to select the folder you want to use as a virtual directory.

Enter an **Alias** name.

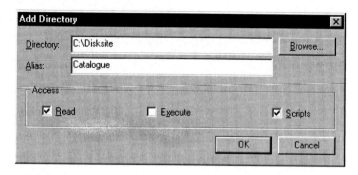

In the **Access** frame you must activate the **Scripts** check box to allow the server to run scripts from this directory.

Click **OK**.

*To modify the properties of a virtual directory, select the directory concerned and click the **Edit Properties** button (the **Edit Directory** dialog box is similar to the **Add Directory** dialog box).*

*Your virtual directory appears as /**Alias**, for example: /Catalogue.*

Managing your ColdFusion server

You must start your application server, after starting your Personal Web Server.

Click the **Start** button and select **Programs - ColdFusion Server - ColdFusion** then click **Coldfusion Administrator**.

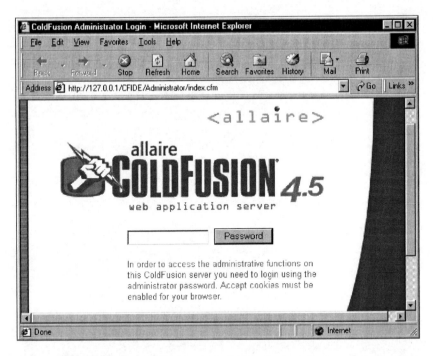

Enter your **Password** to access the ColdFusion server administration console.

*The **data sources** menu of this console allows you to manage your database connections using ODBC, OLE DB or Native drivers.*

Managing your JRun (JSP) server

You must start your application server after you start your Personal Web Server.

Click the **Start** button and select **Programs - JRun 3.0 - JRun Admin Server** then click **JRun Default Server**.

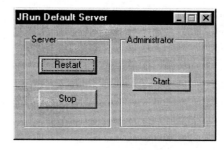

⊡ In the **Administrator** frame, click the **Start** button.

*JRun opens an **html** page.*

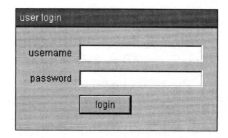

⊡ Enter your **username** and **password** and click the **login** button.

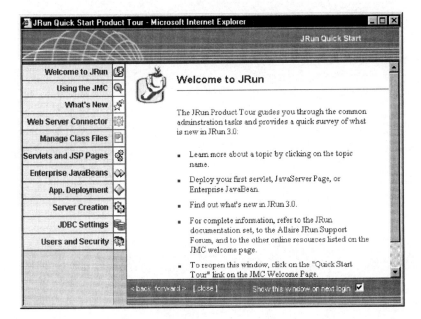

*The **JRun Quick Start Product Tour** window provides an overview of the main procedures you need to follow to administer your server.*

You can manage your JDBS data sources, modify the configuration of your http server and install EJBs (Enterprise JavaBeans):

Introduction

To use the UltraDev interface, you need to have installed it by running the UltraDev installer from the Dreamweaver UltraDev CD-ROM.

The UltraDev interface is based on two specific windows: the **Server behaviors** window and the **Data Bindings** window.

The **Server Behaviors** window generates server-side ASP, JSP and ColdFusion scripts that allow you to connect to databases, extract data and work on sessions and cookies, for example.

The **Data Bindings** window allows you to insert and format dynamic data in your results page.

UltraDev windows

Server Behaviors window

This is the main UltraDev window. It allows you to choose behaviours for the server model you have selected (ASP, JSP or ColdFusion).

Window
Server Behaviors

Ctrl F9 (PC)
⌘ ⌘ F9 (Mac)

Here is the **Server Behaviors** menu for the **ASP** server model:

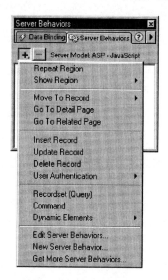

Here is the **Server Behaviors** menu for **JSP** server model:

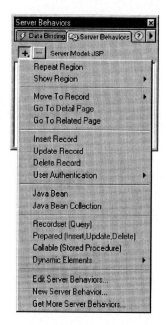

Here is the **Server Behaviors** menu for **Coldfusion** server model:

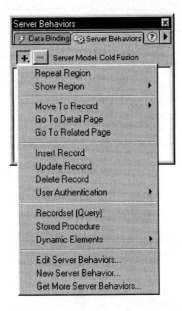

 To use all the features the UltraDev application offers, you may need to enhance your knowledge of ASP, JSP and ColdFusion.

Data Bindings window

This window allows you to insert dynamic data into your html page after you have defined a server behaviour.

 **Window**
Data Bindings

 (PC)
(Mac)

*Alternatively, you can select the **Data Bindings** tab of the **Server Behaviors** window.*

*The **Data Bindings** window is empty by default. You must define a server behavior before you can insert data into your page.*

You can also access the **Server Behaviors** or the **Data Bindings** window using the **Launcher Bar**:

or the **Mini-Launcher**:

 In all the UltraDev windows and dialog boxes, the lightning bolt icon always symbolises dynamic data insertion.

Objects panel

You can insert live objects in a page in two ways: you can use the **Insert - Live - Objects** menu or you can use the **Objects** panel.

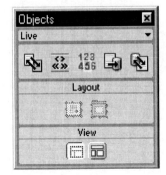

You can insert the following live objects:

  Master-Detail Page Set

  Recordset Navigation Bar

  Recordset Navigation Status

  Record Insertion Form

  Record Update Form.

Introduction

Before you define your site, you must indicate the application server you want to use: ASP, JSP or ColdFusion. As with the standard version of Dreamweaver, UltraDev allows you to manage all your Web application files.

To configure your Web site, you must:

— indicate where you want to store your files,

— specify a server technology (ASP, JSP or ColdFusion),

— define the URL for working in LiveData mode,

— define the address of any remote Web site that accommodates your pages.

Defining your site

⊡ **Site**
New Site

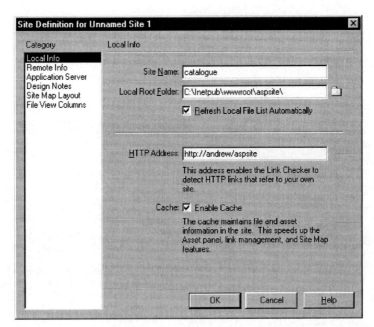

Local Info category

 Enter a name for your site in the **Site Name** box.

 In the **Local Root Folder** box, indicate the access path to the folder that contains the files for your Web application.

It is preferable to create your dynamic sites in the root directory of the Personal Web Server, **C:\Inetpub\wwwroot**: for example, **C:\Inetpub\wwwroot\ mywebsite**.

If the folder that contains your pages is not in the server root directory, you must create a virtual directory (see the **Managing your personal Web server** section of the **Local Web server** chapter).

 In the **HTTP Address** box, enter the address of your Web site, if you want to use the Link Checker for your site.

Remote Info category

 The **Remote Info** category allows you to specify the online access settings for your site.

 The **Access** pop-up menu allows you to indicate the local or remote access for your site:

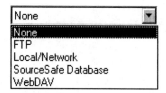

None   This option allows you to test your site locally.

FTP   This option allows you to manage online FTP access to your remote server. Your account manager will provide the necessary information for connecting to your Web site (host name, identifier and password).

Local/Network   This option allows you to manage your site either on your computer or on a local network (Windows network drive or Macintosh AppleTalk server).

SourceSafe Database   This option allows you to connect to databases and SourceSafe servers (Microsoft). In this case, click the **Settings** button and enter the necessary information for accessing your SourceSafe database.

WebDav   This option allows you to manage WebDav (Web-based Distributed authoring and versioning). Click the **Settings** button and enter your WebDav connection information.

↴ According to the **Access** option you choose, you must define certain settings (see below).

Remote Info category: FTP settings

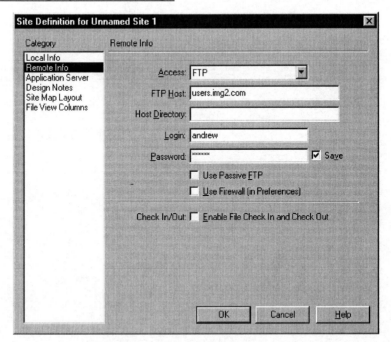

Define the settings:

FTP Host   Specify the FTP address of your site.

Host Directory   Specify the name of the folder that contains your Web application server on the remote server.

Login   Enter your login name.

Password   Enter your password.

Use Passive FTP   Activate this option in the case of a passive connection.

Use Firewall   Activate this option if necessary: by default, it specifies an access on the Firewall port 21 (**Edit - Preferences - Site** category).

Check with your accounts manager whether you must activate one or both of these options.

Use the **Connects to remote host icon** 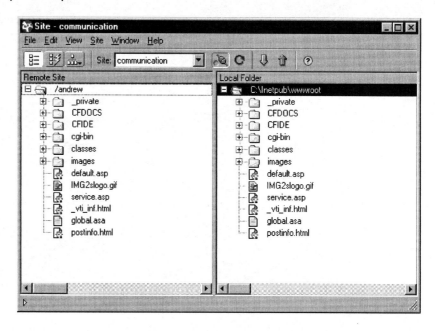 *to access your remote server and manage file transfer:*

It is better to use the same file hierarchy for the local site and the remote site.

Remote Info category: Local/Network access settings

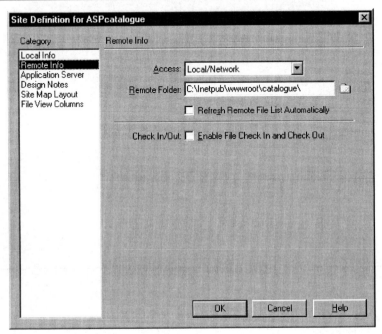

⊡ Define the settings:

Remote Folder Specify the local or remote folder that accommodates your Web application files.

Refresh Remote File List Automatically Activate this option to update the remote file list automatically.

Check In/Out Activate the **Enable File Check in and Check Out** option to manage team work.

 To update the remote file list, choose **View - Refresh Remote** (PC) or **Site - View Site Files - Refresh Remote** (Mac).

Application Server category

The **Application Server** category allows you to set up your application server.

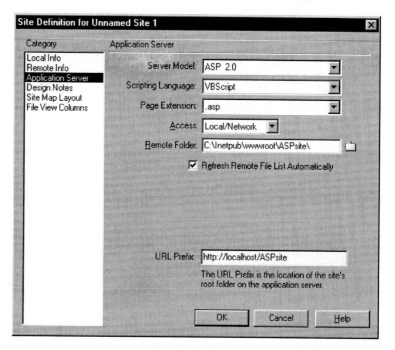

⊡ Define your settings:

Server Model　　Choose ASP 2.0, JSP 1.0 or Cold Fusion 4.0.

Scripting Language　Choose a scripting language according to your server model. For an ASP server you can choose either **JavaScript** or **VBScript**. **JSP** technology uses the Java language and ColdFusion technology uses the **CFML** language.

Page Extension　　Choose the name extension for your dynamic pages. The default choice is **.asp** for ASP, **.jsp** for JSP and **.cfm** for ColdFusion.

Access　　Choose the type of access.

URL Prefix   Enter the URL of your Web site. UltraDev uses this information when you use LiveData view or preview your site in a browser.

 Click **OK** to confirm your settings and close your dialog box.

The **Site** *window appears.*

To change the settings for a site, choose **Site - Defines Sites**.

Introduction

Before you can query and manage database information, you must create a database connection. To set up a database connection, you must define the following settings:

- the driver for accessing your database (for example: MS Access, SQL Server or Oracle),
- the folder or server that accommodates the data,
- the data access permissions.

With Dreamweaver UltraDev, you can connect most commercially available databases to your Web site via ODBC (Open DataBase Connectivity), via a specific connection string (OLE DB, DSN-less) or via JDBC (Java DataBase Connectivity) for JSP.
You can also define a local connection or a connection to the remote application server.
Macintosh users must define connections to the remote application server.

Defining an ODBC connection for ASP

ODBC (Open DataBase Connectivity) is a standard technology that allows you to communicate with a large number of databases. In fact, most commercially available databases provide an ODBC driver. When you define an ODBC connection, you must give a DSN (Data Source Name) to your data source: to activate an ODBC connection you must use the DSN and not the database name.

⊡ In the main **UltraDev** window, open the **Modify** menu and choose the **Connections** option.

A dialog box appears, listing any connections you have set up previously:

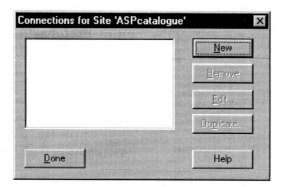

Click the **New** button and choose the **Data Source Name (DSN)** option:

Click the **Define** button.

*This button starts up the **ODBC Data Source Administrator** (you can also access this tool from the **Control Panel**).*

Select the **System DNS** tab.

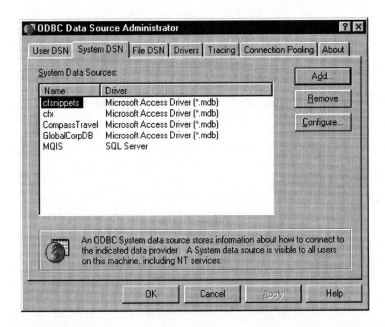

↵ Click the **Add** button and choose a database driver (**Microsoft Access Driver**, for example):

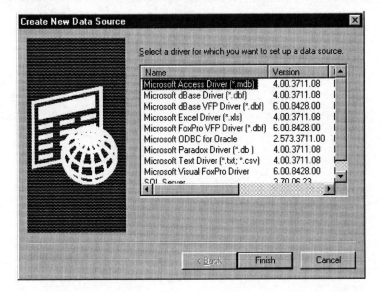

⊡ Click the **Finish** button.

In the final step, you must enter a name for your data source and choose a database.

⊡ In the **Data Source Name** box, enter the name of your data source (catalogue, for example).

For an ODBC data source, it is generally convenient to use the database name (without an extension).

⊡ Click the **Select** button to indicate the access path to the database (make sure you click the database file to select it). If you are working with the Personal Web Server, the access path of your database will be a subfolder of C:\Inetpub\wwwroot for version 4.0, or of C:\Webshare\wwwroot for previous versions.

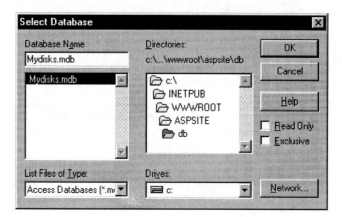

⊡ Click **OK**.

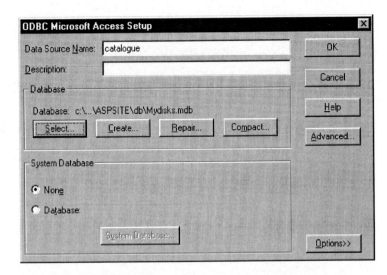

*The name of your database appears in the **Database** frame.*

⊡ Click **OK**.

*Your database appears in the **System Data Sources** list:*

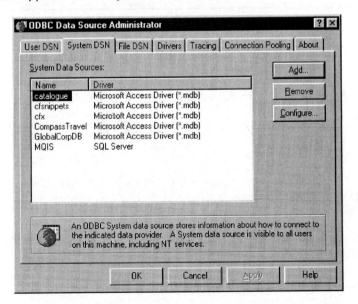

Click **OK**.

You return to the ***Data Source Name (DSN)*** *dialog box.*

In the **Connection Name** box, enter the name of your connection (Catalo-gueConnection, for example):

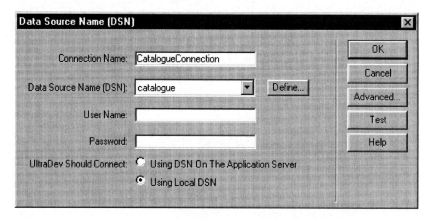

UltraDev will create a ***Connections*** *folder in your site. It will generate the ASP script to connect to your data source and insert this script in the page via an SSI (Server Side Include).*

```
<!--#includefile="Connections/catalogueconnection.asp" -->
```

UltraDev sets up the connection to the database, once and for all. When you create a new recordset, you select the connection name directly from the ***Connections*** *list.*

The **User Name** and the **Password** are optional. Enter them, if necessary.

Choose one of the **UltraDev Should Connect** options:

Using DSN On The Application Server: activate this option to use a data source on a remote server (if you cannot create a DSN on your local computer, for example).

Using Local DSN: activate this option to use a data source on your local computer.

Click the **Test** button to test the connection to your database:

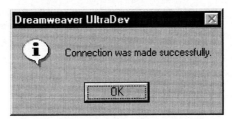

 You can create a new connection or modify an existing connection at any time, using the **Modify - Connections** menu option.

Creating a DSN-less connection for ASP

You can connect to a database via ODBC without creating a DSN data source: this is called a DSN-less connection. For this purpose, you must set up a custom connection string according to the database you will use. Consult the your database's documentation for the exact syntax you must use for the connection.

Open the **Modify** menu and choose the **Connections** option.

A dialog box appears, listing any connections you have set up previously:

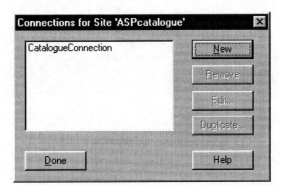

☐ Click the **New** button and choose the **Custom Connection String** option:

> Custom Connection String
> Data Source Name (DSN)

☐ Enter a **Connection Name** (do not use any special characters).

☐ Enter the **Connection String** corresponding to your database.

For example, here is the format of a connection string for an **Access 2000** database:

Driver={Microsoft Access Driver (*.mdb)}; DBQ=c:\access_path\db.mdb

Here is the format of a connection string for an **SQL Server** database:

Driver={SQL Server}; Server=server_name; Database=database_name; UID=user_name; PWD=user_password

Here is the DSN-less **Connection String** for an MS Access 2000 database called disks.mdb that resides in the Personal Web Server directory:

Driver={Microsoft Access Driver (*.mdb)}; DBQ=c:\inetpub\wwwroot\catalogue\disks.mdb

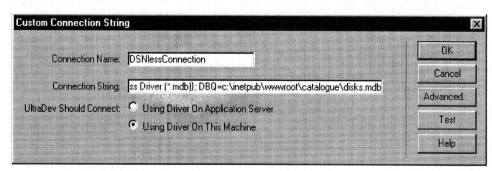

☐ Choose one of the **Ultradrev Should Connect** options:

Using Driver On Application Server Activate this option to use a data source on a remote server (you must have previously configured the access to the remote access server: see the **Defining a site** chapter).

Using Driver On This Machine Activate this option to use a data source on your local computer.

⊡ Click the **Test** button to test the connection to your database:

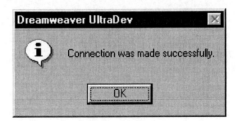

Defining an OLE DB connection for ASP

OLE DB connections access databases quicker than ODBC connections, as the OLE DB provider communicates directly with the database. For a Microsoft Access or SQL Server database, you will need the OLE DB components. For this purpose you must install the latest version of MDAC (Microsoft Data Access Components). You can download MDAC from the Microsoft Web site, to be sure you have the latest version.

⊡ Open the **Modify** menu and choose the **Connections** option.

A dialog box appears, listing any connections you have set up previously:

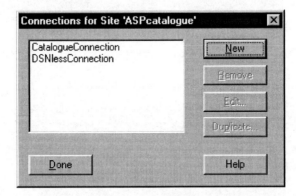

⊡ Click the **New** button and choose the **Custom Connection String** option:

⊡ Enter the **Connection Name**.

⊡ Enter the OLE DB **Connection String** corresponding to your database.

Here is the format of a connection string for an **Access 2000** database:
Provider=Microsoft.Jet.OLEDB.4.0; Data Source=c:\path\to\database.mdb
(make sure you indicate the absolute path).

Here is the format of a connection string for an **SQL Server** database:
Provider=SQLOLEDB; Data Source=server_name; Initial Catalog=database_name; User ID=user_name; Password=user_password

Here is the OLE DB connection string for an MS Access 2000 database called disks.mdb that resides in the Personal Web Server directory, c:\inetpub\wwwroot\catalogue\:

Provider=Microsoft.Jet.OLEDB.4.0; Data Source =c:\inetpub\wwwroot\catalogue\disks.mdb

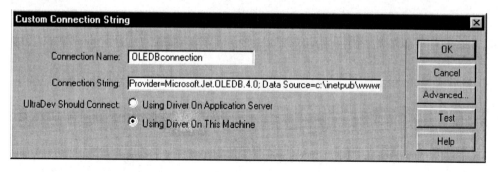

⊡ Choose one of the **Ultradev Should Connect** options:

Using Driver On Application Server
Activate this option to use a data source on a remote server.

Using Driver On This Machine
Activate this option to use a data source on your local computer.

Click the **Test** button to test the connection to your database:

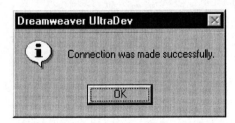

Using Server.MapPath for an ASP connection

You can create a connection using a relative access path to the data. The ASP object, Server.MapPath forwards to the connection string the absolute path of your ASP pages on the server. This approach helps you to manage your site hierarchy.

You can use this technique with DSN-less or OLE DB connections.

For a **DSN-less connection with Ms Access**, enter your **Custom Connection String** in the following format:
Driver={Microsoft Access Driver (*.mdb)}; DBQ=" & Server.Mappath ("\relative_path\db.mdb")

For example, for an MS Access 2000 database called disks.mdb in a site sub-folder called db:
Driver={Microsoft Access Driver (*.mdb)}; DBQ=" & Server.Mappath ("\db\disks.mdb")

For an **OLE DB connection with MS Access**, enter your **Custom Connection String** in the following format:
Provider={Microsoft.Jet.OLEDB.4.0; Data Source=" & Server.Mappath ("\relative_path\db.mdb")

For example, for an MS Access 2000 database called disks.mdb in a site sub-folder called db:
Provider={Microsoft.Jet.OLEDB.4.0; Data Source=" & Server.Mappath ("\db\disks.mdb")

Important note: In the **Custom Connection String** dialog box, you must activate the **Using Driver On Application Server** option. To test your connection string, you need an active Internet connection to the remote application server.

Defining an ODBC connection for ColdFusion

⊡ In the **Modify** menu and choose the **Connections** option.

A dialog box appears, listing any connections have been set up previously:

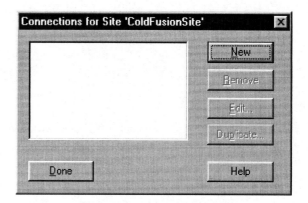

⊡ Click the **New** button and choose the **Data Source Name** option:

⊟ If this is the first connection you are creating for the site, UltraDev asks you to enter the RDS login information. Click the **Login** button and enter the **User Name** and **Password** of the RDS ColdFusion server administrator. This information allows UltraDev to obtain the list of data sources defined on the ColdFusion server:

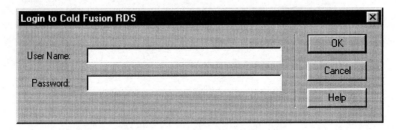

⊟ Click the **OK** button.

⊟ Choose a DSN from the **Data Source Name (DSN)** pop-up menu.

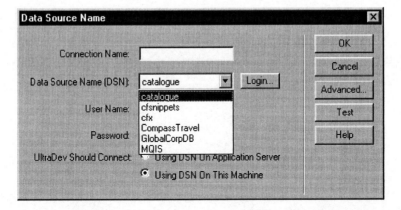

⊟ Enter a **Connection Name**.

⊟ If necessary, enter a **User NAME** and **Password**.

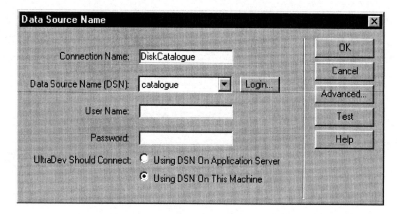

⊟ Choose one of the **UltraDev Should Connect** options:

Using DSN On Application Server   Activate this option to use a data source on a remote server (if you cannot create a DSN on your local computer, for example).

Using DSN on This Machine   Activate this option to use a data source on your local computer.

⊟ Click the **Test** button to test the connection to your database:

*UltraDev will create a **Connections** folder in your site. It will generate the ColdFusion script to connect to your data source and insert this script in the page via an SSI (Server Side Include).*

```
<cfinclude template="Connections/DiskCatalogue.cfm">
```

Defining a JDBC connection for ColdFusion

⊡ Open the **Modify** menu and choose the **Connections** option.

A dialog box appears, listing any connections you have set up previously:

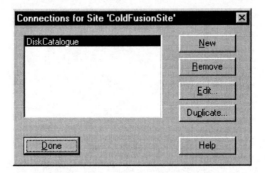

⊡ Click the **New** button and choose the **Data Source Name - Advanced** option:

⊡ Enter a **Connection Name**.

⊡ Open the **Data Source Name (DSN)** list and choose the DSN to use.

⊡ If necessary, enter a **User Name** and **Password**.

⊡ Define the JDBC connection **Driver**: for example, the Sun JDBC-ODBC Bridge driver: **sun.jdbc.odbc.JdbcOdbcDriver**.

⊡ In the **URL** box, enter the name of the DSN used: for example **jdbc:odbc:catalogue**, where **catalogue** is the name of the ODBC data source.

⊡ If necessary, enter a **User Name** and **Password**.

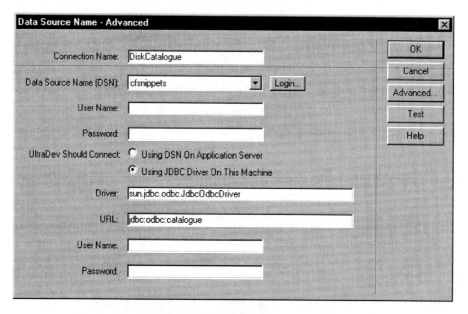

⊡ Click the **Test** button to test the connection to your database:

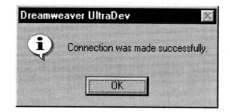

Defining a JDBC connection for JSP

JDBC (Java Database Connectivity) is the Java equivalent of ODBC. To communicate with ODBC, you can define a JDBC connection using a specific driver or using a JDBC-ODBC bridge driver (for example, Sun's JDBC-ODBC Bridge driver).

⊡ In the **Modify** menu, choose the **Connections** option.

A dialog box appears, listing any connections you have set up previously:

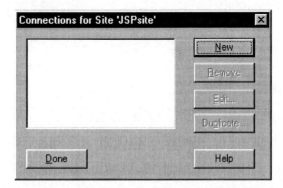

⊡ Click the **New** button and choose the **Driver** corresponding to your database and to the type of connection you want to set up. For example, to set up a connection via ODBC, you could choose the **Sun JDBC-ODBC Driver (ODBC Database)**:

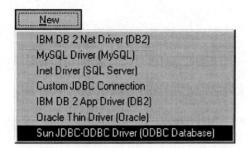

⊡ UltraDev automatically generates the contents of the **Driver** text box. It gives an example of the syntax required in the **URL** box.

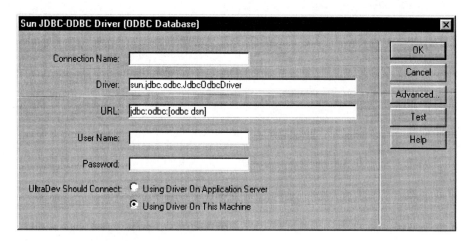

⊡ Enter a **Connection Name**.

⊡ In the **URL** box, enter the name of the DSN used: for example **jdbc:odbc:catalogue**, where **catalogue** is the name of the ODBC data source.

⊡ If necessary, enter a **User Name** and **Password**.

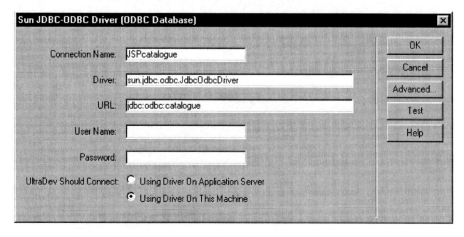

Click the **Test** button to test the connection to your database:

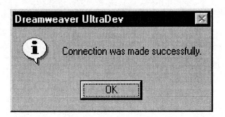

UltraDev will create a **Connections** folder in your site. It will generate the JSP script to connect to your data source and insert this script in the page via an SSI (Server Side Include).

```
<%@ include file="Connections/DiskCatalogue.jsp" %>
```

Modifying a connection

 Modify
Connections

*The **Connections** dialog box appears.*

 Choose an action:

New   to create a new connection,

Remove   to delete a connection,

Edit   to modify a connection (you can change the connection settings, but not the connection name),

Duplicate   to make a copy of a connection.

Restricting the amount of ASP, JSP or ColdFusion information

*While you are developping dynamic pages, your databases tend to contain large amounts of information or specific data that the application cannot handle. If this is the case, you will need to limit the number of items you show. For this purpose, you can create a **schema** or a **catalog** in your database.*

 You cannot create a **schema** or a **catalog** with Microsoft Access.

⊡ **Modify**
Connections

⊡ Select the connection to modify.

⊡ Click the **Modify** button.

*The **Connections** dialog box appears.*

⊡ Click the **Advanced** button.

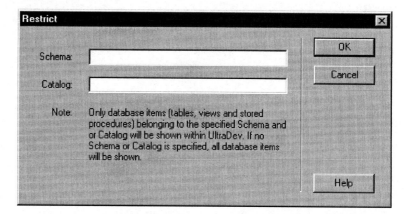

⊡ Enter the names of your **Schema** and your **Catalog**.

⊡ Click the **OK** button.

You can also restrict the number of database items by clicking the **Advanced** button when you create a database connection.

ASP, JSP and ColdFusion Connections folders

UltraDev creates a folder called **Connections** at the root of your site. This folder contains your ASP, JSP or ColdFusion connection files. Each of these files contains the connection settings for your database.
You must download the complete set of site files to your remote application server.

Connecting from a Macintosh

You can define a connection for an ASP, JSP or ColdFusion site, but you must work on the remote server. To indicate to UltraDev that you are using a remote application server, carry out the following steps:

⊟ **Site**
Define Sites

⊟ In the **Application Server** category, the **URL Prefix** box must contain the address of your site.

Connecting via the Recordset dialog box

You can also define a connection when you create a recordset.

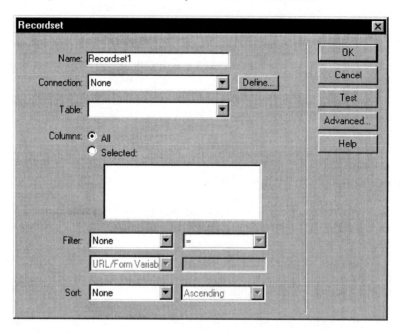

 In the **Recordset** dialog box, click the **Define** button to the right of the **Connection** box. In the **Connections** dialog box that appears, define your connection, as described above.

Here are the main ways of interacting with a database:

— by running a query with one or more search conditions from a search form,

— by extracting information from a cookie or a session variable,

— by restricting or customizing access to a site via a user name and a password stored in the database,

— by adding, updating or deleting information in a database,

— by linking a main page that contains all the extracted data and a page that shows detailed information concerning a specific database record.

You use UltraDev in the same way, irrespective of the database you are using: MS Access, SQL Server, Oracle or any other database. In all cases, you must create a recordset and change its settings to suit your purpose.

Here are the steps you must follow:

— define a database connection (See the **Connecting to databases** chapter),

— specify the fields to extract and the database search conditions,

— insert the data from your recordset into your results page,

— format your results page,

— check that your page works properly.

Creating a recordset

A recordset is the set of data you extract when you run an SQL (Structured Query Language) query on a database. You can use SQL with most commercially available databases. SQL is a simple and powerful means of extracting, deleting and updating information.

You use the same techniques, whether you are developing in ASP, JSP or ColdFusion. However, each of these technologies has a slightly different approach to creating a database connection.

You do not need to know SQL to create a recordset in simple mode. On the other hand, in advanced mode UltraDev allows you to write your own SQL queries (see the **Introducing SQL** chapter).

⊡ Open the **Server Behaviors** window.

⊡ Click the ⊞ button to add a server behaviour.

Choose the **Recordset (Query)** option.

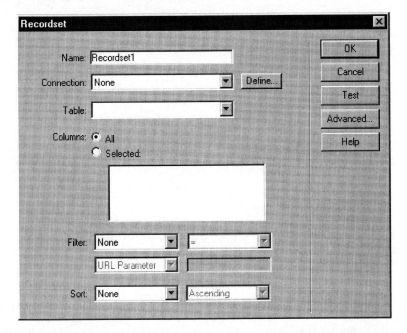 To create a recordset, you must have previously specified the type of Web server you want to use. If you have not yet done so, UltraDev displays the **Application Server** site definition dialog box (see the **Defining a site** chapter for how to set up your server model).

*The **Recordset** dialog box comprises two parts. In the upper part, you must enter the **Name** of your recordset and either select or **Define** your **Connection** to a database.*

*In the lower part (**Filter**) you can structure your query and indicate how UltraDev must transmit the parameters: via a search form, a URL, a cookie or a (fixed) entered value.*

If you have not yet created a database connection, UltraDev reminds you that you must do so before you can create a recordset.

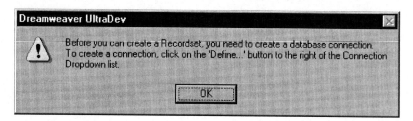

*To create a new database connection, click the **Define** button, to the right of the **Connection** box. Alternatively, you can use the **Modify - Connections** menu option.*

Setting up a recordset

*Once you have created your database connection, you can select the fields you want to extract from your database and structure your SQL query. By default, the **Recordset** dialog box is in simple mode and you do not need to know SQL to set up your query.*

In simple mode you can create a query with a single condition.

⊡ In the **Name** field, enter the name of your recordset (for example, **Results**).

 Do not use any spaces or special characters in your recordset name.

⊡ Choose a database connection from the **Connection** drop-down list.

UltraDev activates the connection and reads the list of tables that your database contains.

⊡ Select a table or a view from the **Table** drop-down list (for an MS Access database, for example, this list shows the full set of tables and views in the database).

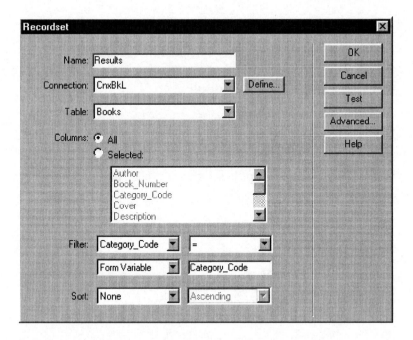

*The corresponding list of fields appears in the list under **Columns**.*

☐ Choose a **Columns** option:

All   to extract all the fields.

Selected   to select from the list the fields you want to extract:
                      use the `Shift` key to select several adjacent fields; use the
                      `Ctrl` key (PC) or the `⌘ ⌦` key (Mac) to select several
                      non-adjacent fields.

 To improve the performance of your site, select only those fields you need.

Defining a filter

*In the **Recordset** dialog box, the **Filter** list allows you to set up your query to extract data from your database. For example, you may want to extract from the **Books** table in the classics (**CLA**) category.*

UltraDev will automatically generate the SQL code for your query.

You must define your filter in four steps:

In the first drop-down list, choose the **field** you want to use for your condition.

Next, choose the relational operator:

=	equal to
>	greater than
<	less than
>=	greater than or equal to
<=	less than or equal to
<>	not equal to

begins with

ends with

contains

In the third drop-down list, underneath the first drop-down list, choose the query mechanism you want to use:

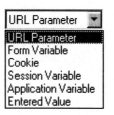

URL Parameter	Choose this option if you want to send the search condition via a form using the GET method.
Form Variable	Choose this option if you want to send the search condition via a form using the POST method.
Cookie	Choose this option to obtain the search condition via a cookie.
Session Variable	Choose this option if you want to send the search condition via a session variable.
Application Variable	Choose this option if you want to send the search condition via an application variable.
Entered Value	Choose this option if you want to use a (fixed) entered value as the search condition.

⊟ In the fourth **Filter** box, enter a name for your variable. UltraDev will use this variable to store the condition value and build the search condition. UltraDev can get this value from a form field, a cookie, a session or an application. UltraDev will generate the ASP, JSP or ColdFusion scripts according to your specification.

*For example: suppose you want to query a book list. You could choose the **Classics** condition in a form that searches according to book category.*
*UltraDev will obtain the **Classics** value in a form variable then generate the SQL query using the condition: **Category = Classics**.*

⊟ In the first **Sort** drop-down list, indicate the order in which you want to sort the recordset:

Ascending   1, 2, 3...   A, B, C...
Descending   in reverse order.

⊟ Click the **Test** button to test your query.

For example, suppose your database provides a book list that contains a **Category -Code** field with a number of values, including **CLA** (Classics), **CMP** (Computing), **CRI** (Crime), **FIC** (Fiction) and **HIS** (History) and that UltraDev will send one of these values via a search form. If you enter **CLA** in the **Test Value** field, UltraDev will simulate the extraction from the database according to your condition and return the query result.

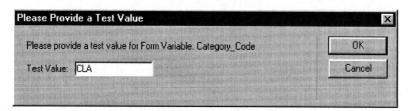

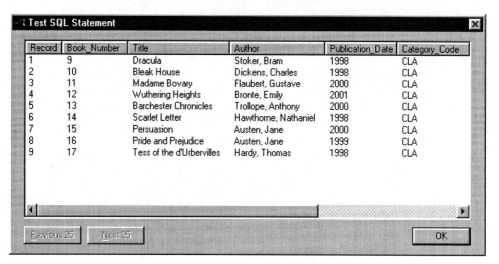

If your condition test reveals no errors, but your search form does not work on the server, the problem may well be due to the field names in your form.

Creating a recordset in advanced mode

In advanced mode, you must write your query in SQL and define all the form, session, application and cookie variables you use.

Advanced mode allows you to create more sophisticated queries, but you need to know the scripting languages for the server technology you are using.

⊟ In the **Recordset** dialog box, click the **Advanced** button. Define your variables and their execution values.

⊟ In the **SQL** box, you can enter your query directly (see the **Introducing SQL** chapter). Alternatively, you can use the graphic editor in the lower part of the dialog box:

— In the **Database Items** box, view the list(s) of fields by expanding the **Tables** branch followed by the table(s) or view(s) concerned. Select the field(s) you want to extract, one after the other, by clicking the **SELECT** button after choosing each field: UltraDev adds each field you select to the **SELECT** statement in the **SQL** frame.

— Choose the fields for which you want to define a comparison condition and click the **WHERE** button after each of them.

*UltraDev adds each field you choose, to the **WHERE** clause of the **SELECT** statement in the format: **WHERE field** for the first field or **AND field** for subsequent fields.*

— Choose the field you want to use to sort the data and click the **ORDER BY** button.

For example:

SELECT Author, Title, Publication_Date WHERE Category_Code='CLA' ORDER BY Author

*This query, which is based on the **Books** table, extracts the name of the author, the title and the publication date for books in the Classics category (whose code is **CLA**). The result is sorted in ascending order according to author.*

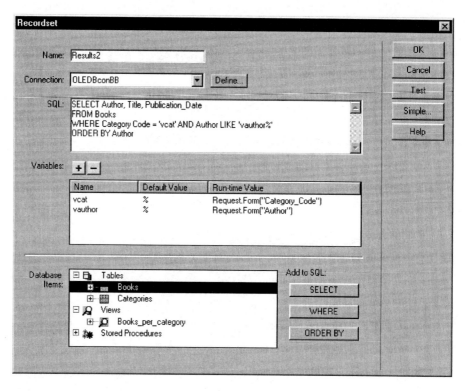

 To insert variables, use the **Variables** box:

    — Click the **+** button to define your variable in the **Name** column.

    — In the second column, enter its **Default Value**.

    — In the final column, enter its **Run-time Value**.

    — Repeat each of these steps for each variable you want to create.

You must define your variables before you create your SQL query.

Click the **Test** button to check that your SQL query gives the results you expect: next, you can insert the dynamic data in your results page.

Here are examples of variable declarations for ASP, JSP and ColdFusion:

Server Model	Name	Default Value	Run-time Value
ASP	vauthor	%	Request("Author")
JSP	vauthor	%	Request.getParameter("Author")
ColdFusion	vauthor	%	#Author#

Using a view in advanced mode

*UltraDev displays the views that your database defines under the **Views** database item. You can use a view as you would use an SQL queries.*

 UltraDev considers a query defined in MS Access to be a view. This approach allows you to run a query directly from a dynamic page.

↰ In the **Recordset** dialog box, expand the **Views** branch in the **Database Items** box.

UltraDev displays the names of the views and their associated fields.

↰ Expand a view, choose the fields you want to insert in the SQL query and click the **SELECT** button after each of them.

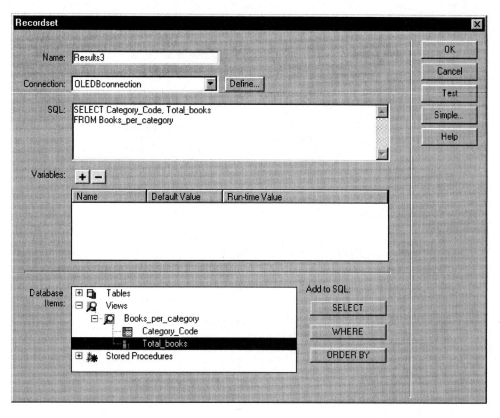

⊡ Click the **Test** button to check that your SQL query gives the results you expect: next, you can insert the dynamic data in your results page.

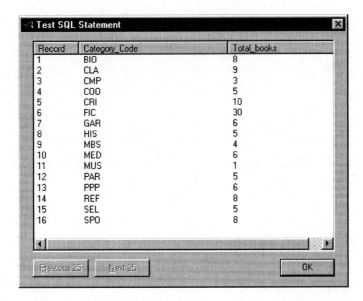

Using stored procedures in advanced mode

In the **Recordset** dialog box (in **Advanced** mode), expand the **Stored Procedures** branch in the **Database Items** box.

Choose the stored procedure you want to use and click the **Procedures** button. If necessary, enter any parameter values the stored procedure requires.

Modifying a recordset

In the **Server Behaviors** window, double-click the **Recordset** you want to modify.

*The **Recordset** dialog box appears: you can carry out your modifications.*

Modifying the properties of a recordset

 In the **Server Behaviors** window, select the **Recordset** whose properties you want to modify then choose the **Window - Properties** menu option to display the property inspector.

 Choose the property you want to modify (ASP, JSP, ColdFusion):

— the name of the recordset in the **Recordset** box,

— the database **Connection**, by clicking the **Edit** button,

— the recordset query, in the **SQL** box.

To modify certain properties, particularly the SQL property, you need a sound knowledge of the technology used: ASP, JSP or ColdFusion.

Defining the ASP cursor type

The cursor determines how you can move through the data in a recordset. A recordset object can have one of four types of cursor.

 In the **Property inspector**, choose the **Cursor Type** :

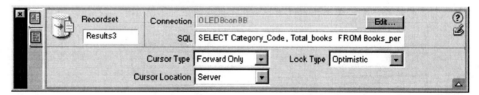

Forward Only (adOpenForwardOnly)	This cursor type allows you to move through the data in a forward direction only (this is the fastest cursor type).
Keyset (adOpenKeyset)	This cursor type allows you to move through the data in both directions, but you will not be able to view any records that other users may add while you are consulting the data.

Dynamic
(adOpenDynamic)

This cursor type allows you to move through the data in both directions. In addition, you will be able to view any records that other users may add while you are consulting the data.

Static
(adOpenStatic)

This cursor type allows you to move through the data in both directions. It creates a static copy of the recordset. You will be able to view any records that other users may add, delete or modify while you are consulting the data.

The **Lock Type** specifies whether or not a record can be modified:

Read Only
(adLockReadOnly)

The data cannot be modified.

Pessimistic
(adLockPessimistic)

The data is locked, record by record.

Optimistic
(adLockOptimistic)

The records are locked, one after the other, as the database is backed-up.

BatchOptimistic
(adLockBatchOptimistic)

The records are updated batch by batch.

Choose the cursor location from the **Cursor Location** list (**Client** or **Server**).

Defining the types of recordset in JSP

The recordset type determines the type of cursor (how you can scroll throught the data in the recordset).

In the recordset's property inspector, choose the **Recordset Type**:

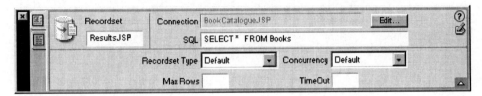

Forward Only
(ResultSet.TYPE_FORWARD_ONLY)

This cursor type allows you to move through the data in a forward direction only (this is the fastest cursor type).

Scroll Sensitive
(ResultSet.TYPE_SCROLL_SENSITIVE)

This cursor type allows you to move through the data in both directions. In addition, you will be able to view any records that other users may add while you are consulting the data.

Scroll Insensitive
(ResultSet.TYPE_SCROLL_INSENSITIVE)

This cursor type allows you to move through the data in both directions, but you will not be able to view any records that other users may add while you are consulting the data.

The **Concurrency** specifies whether or not a record can be modified:

Read Only
(ResultSet.CONCUR_READ_ONLY)

The data cannot be modified.

Updateable
(ResultSet.CONCUR_UPDATEABLE)

The data can be modified.

The **Max Rows (StatementResult.setFetchSize(number_of_rows))** field indicates to the JDBC driver the number of rows the database must return.

The **TimeOut (StatementResult.setQueryTimeout(seconds))** field allows you to set a maximum time to wait for a query to run.

Defining the number of rows in ColdFusion

In the recordset's property inspector, the **Max Rows** box allows you to specify the maximum number of rows the database must return. By default, the database returns all the rows.

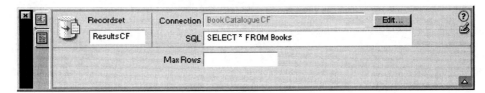

Overview

SQL (Structured Query Language) allows you to select and process records contained in a relational database. With UltraDev, you need to use
SQL to set up a recordset in advanced mode.

Here are the principal SQL statements for handling data:

SELECT   to select data

INSERT   to insert data

UPDATE   to update data

DELETE   to delete data

SELECT statement

Basics

The SELECT statement finds and extracts from a database, a set of records that correspond to one or more conditions.

Here is the basic syntax of a SELECT statement:

```
SELECT field1, field2 ... names of the fields you want to extract
FROM table1, table2 ... names of the tables from which you want
to extract
WHERE search condition(s)
ORDER BY how you want to sort the records
```

You can also use the following syntax to extract fields from a database:

```
SELECT table1.field1, table1.field2, table2.field1, table2.field
```

or **SELECT** *

After the **SELECT** keyword, indicate the list of fields you want to extract: use the **SELECT *** syntax to extract all the fields; use the **SELECT table1.field1**, **table1.field2**... syntax if you have identical field names in different tables. After the **FROM** keyword, indicate the name(s) of the table(s) that contain the data. Important note: if your field names contain spaces, you must specify them between square brackets in your SQL statement. For example, you must specify Client Code as [Client Code].

The **WHERE** clause specifies the search conditions.

The **ORDER BY** clause allows you to indicate the field(s) by which you want to sort your results table. You can sort in ascending order (**ASC**, the default mode) or in descending order (**DESC**).

 SQL statements and keywords are not case sensitive.

Relational operators

Here are the relational operators you can use in the **WHERE** clause:

=	equal to
>	greater than
<	less than
>=	greater than or equal to
<=	less than or equal to
<>	not equal to

Logical operators

Here are the logical operators you can use in the **WHERE** clause:

LIKE   allows you to select data that starts with, ends with or contains a particular character string. You can use the percentage sign (%) as a wildcard operator in your specification.

BETWEEN   allows you to select data within a range of values.

IN   allows you to select data with respect to a list of values.

IS NULL   allows you to select empty fields.

IS NOT NULL allows you to select fields that contain values.

Conjunction operators

The **AND** and **OR** operators allow you to join several conditions in your **WHERE** clause:

AND all the conditions you link with the **AND** operator must be **TRUE**.

OR at least one of the conditions you link with the **OR** operator must be **TRUE**.

NOT reverses the **TRUE/FALSE** value of a condition.

Examples: SQL queries with Microsoft Access

Suppose you want to query a database that contains the list of your clients. Your Clients table contains the following fields: Client_Code, Company_Name, Contact_ Name, Job_Title City and Employees.

The following Access 2000 queries are examples of the SELECT instruction.

In the **Objects** bar, click the **Queries** button then choose to **Create query in Design view**.

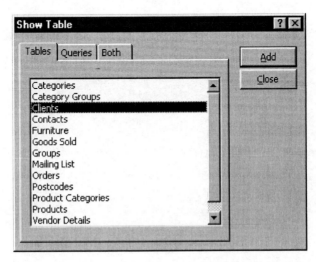

⊡ Click the **Close** button to close the **Show Table** dialog box.

The query design grid is empty.

⊡ Click the SQL ▾ button on the **Query Design** toolbar.

⊡ Enter your SQL query:

For example: suppose you want to extract all the fields for your clients in Westport:

```
SELECT *
FROM Clients
WHERE City ='Westport'
```

⊡ Click the **Run** ▣ button on the **Query Design** toolbar, to run your query.

You obtain a results table equivalent to the recordset you would have obtained in UltraDev:

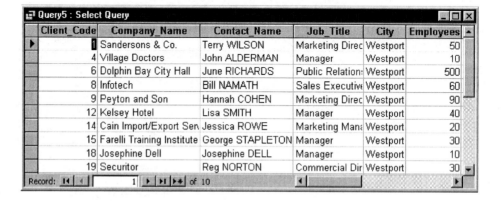

Client_Code	Company_Name	Contact_Name	Job_Title	City	Employees
1	Sandersons & Co.	Terry WILSON	Marketing Direc	Westport	50
4	Village Doctors	John ALDERMAN	Manager	Westport	10
6	Dolphin Bay City Hall	June RICHARDS	Public Relation:	Westport	500
8	Infotech	Bill NAMATH	Sales Executive	Westport	60
9	Peyton and Son	Hannah COHEN	Marketing Direc	Westport	90
12	Kelsey Hotel	Lisa SMITH	Manager	Westport	40
14	Cain Import/Export Sen	Jessica ROWE	Marketing Mana	Westport	20
15	Farelli Training Institute	George STAPLETON	Manager	Westport	30
18	Josephine Dell	Josephine DELL	Manager	Westport	10
19	Securitor	Reg NORTON	Commercial Dir	Westport	30

Record: ◄◄ ◄ 1 ► ►► ►* of 10

To list only the **Client_Code, Company_Name, City** and **Employees** fields for your Westport clients, you could write your query as follows:

```
SELECT Client_Code, Company_Name, City, Employees
FROM Clients
WHERE City ='Westport'
```

You can use the **AND, OR** and **NOT** operators to combine several conditions in your query.

For example, suppose you want to view Westport clients with fewer than 30 employees or fewer:

```
SELECT Employees, Client_Code, Company_Name, City
FROM Clients
WHERE City ='Westport' AND Employees <=30
ORDER BY Employees DESC
```

If a comparison value is text data, you must specify it between apostrophes.

Suppose you want to list your clients in Westport, New Grove and Dryden Bay:

```
SELECT *
FROM Clients
WHERE City ='Westport' OR City ='New Grove' OR City ='Dryden Bay'
```

or

```
WHERE City IN ('Westport' , 'New Grove' , 'Dryden Bay')
```

The **BETWEEN** operator allows you to query your database with respect to a range of values: between a minimum and a maximum value (inclusive).

For example, suppose you want to select your clients that have between 30 and 200 employees:

```
SELECT *
FROM Clients
WHERE Employees >=30 AND Employees <=200
```

or

```
WHERE Employees BETWEEN 30 AND 200
```

 Use the **NOT** operator in your query to exclude any records you do not want. For, example, to list all your clients except those that have between 30 and 200 employees: WHERE Employees NOT BETWEEN 30 AND 200.

You can build more sophisticated queries using the **LIKE** keyword and the wildcard symbol, which symbolises any character string. The standard wildcard symbol is %. However, Microsoft Access also recognises the * character.

For example, you can find the client whose company name begins with "**Inf**", whose contact name ends with "**ton**" or whose company name contains "**and**":

```
SELECT Client_Code, Company_Name, Contact_Name, City
FROM Clients
WHERE Company_Name LIKE 'Inf%'
```

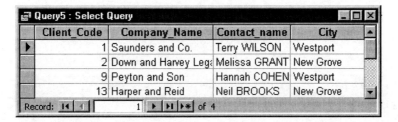

```
WHERE Contact_Name LIKE '%TON'
```

```
WHERE Company_Name LIKE '%and%'
```

To search for data in a date field, you must enter your dates between **#** signs, for example #12/11/2001#.

Suppose you want to extract all your orders between two dates, for example:

```
WHERE Order_Date BETWEEN #1/1/2001# AND #5/4/2001#
```

You can use the **JOIN** keyword to join two tables.

You can write such queries in two ways:

```
SELECT table1.field1, table1.field2, table2.field1, table2.field2
FROM table1 INNER JOIN table2 ON table1.field_name =
table2.field_name
WHERE search_condition(s)
```

or

```
SELECT table1.field1, table1.field2, table2.field1, table2.field2
FROM table1, table2
WHERE table1.field_name = table2.field_name AND search_condition(s)
```

In the **INNER JOIN** clause (1st syntax) or the **WHERE** clause (2nd syntax), you must indicate the field you want to use to link the tables together. You can also specify any search criteria in the **WHERE** clause.

For example, suppose you want to list the orders of all your clients in Westport. The **Clients** and **Orders** tables are linked by a one-to-many relationship on the **Client_Code** field:

```
SELECT *
FROM Clients, Orders
WHERE Clients.Client_Code = Orders.Client_Code AND City = 'Westport'
```

The **DISTINCT** keyword allows you to eliminate duplicates.

For example, suppose you want to list all the cities where you have clients. You want to include each city in your recordset, only once:

```
SELECT DISTINCT City
FROM Clients
```

INSERT statement

Basics

The **INSERT** statement allows you to add records into a database. Here is the basic syntax of an **INSERT** statement:

```
INSERT INTO table (field1, field2...)
VALUES (value1, value2...)
```

After the **INSERT INTO** keywords, you must specify the name of the table, followed by the field names between brackets.

After the **VALUES** keyword, you must indicate the corresponding values between brackets.

For example, suppose you want to insert a new client into your database:

```
INSERT INTO Clients (Company_Name, Contact_Name, Job_Title, City,
Employees)
Values ('PLJ Consultants', 'Bill Simpson', 'Managing Director',
'Westport', 60)
```

When you run this query in MS Access, the following message appears:

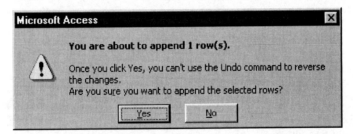

Here is a part of the results table (in this example "Client_Code" was not specified as it is an AutoNumber field, which Access generates automatically):

	Client_Code	Company_Name	Contact_Name	Job_Title	City	Employees
+	16	IPG	Louise MILLER	Commercial Dir	St Lucia	600
+	17	Junger Plastics	Rosemary BRIGHT	Marketing Direc	New Grove	300
+	18	Josephine Dell	Josephine DELL	Manager	Westport	10
+	19	Securitor	Reg NORTON	Commercial Dir	Westport	30
+	20	PLJ Consultants	Bill Simpson	Managing Direc	Westport	60

Record: ◄◄ ◄ 1 ► ►► ►* of 20

You must provide a value for each field you specify in your INSERT statement. Otherwise, the ODBC driver will return an error message when you try to run your query on your server.

UPDATE statement

Basics

The **UPDATE** statement allows you to modify one or more fields in your database. Here is the basic syntax of the **UPDATE** statement:

```
UPDATE table
SET field = value
WHERE condition
```

Indicate the table you want to modify. After the **SET** keyword, specify the field you want to modify with its new value. The **WHERE** clause is optional. It allows you to apply your modification only to the subset of records that meet a certain condition.

Suppose you want to modify the job title of one of your contacts, for example:

```
UPDATE Clients
SET Job_Title = 'Sales Director'
WHERE Contact_Name = 'Neil Brooks'
```

When you run this query in MS Access the following message appears:

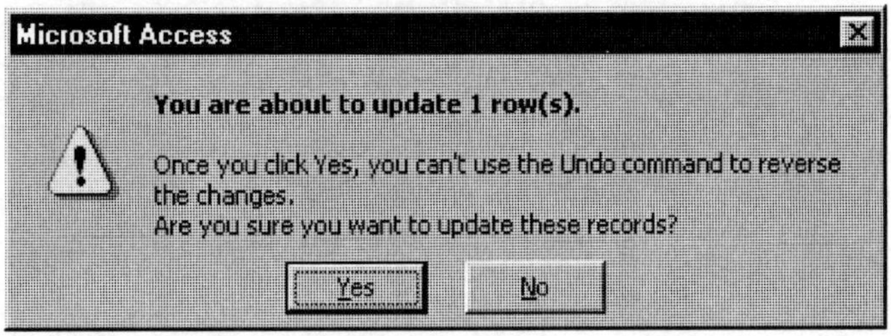

Here is the results table:

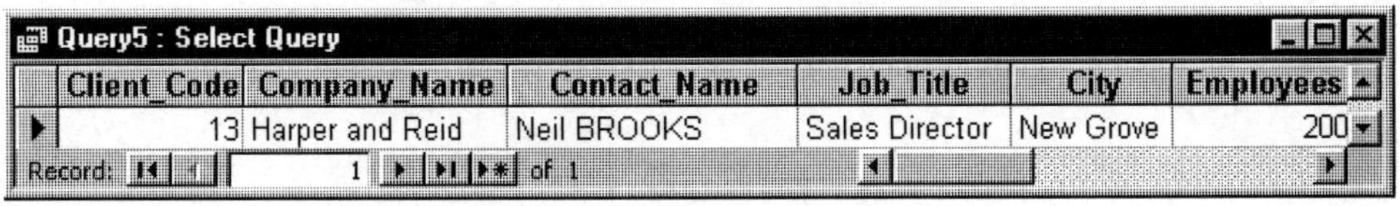
Query5 : Select Query

Client_Code	Company_Name	Contact_Name	Job_Title	City	Employees
13	Harper and Reid	Neil BROOKS	Sales Director	New Grove	200

Record: 1 of 1

DELETE statement

Basics

The **DELETE** statement allows you to delete one or more records from your database. Here is the basic syntax of the **DELETE** statement:

```
DELETE FROM table
WHERE condition
```

You need indicate only the table and the record(s) you want to delete.

Suppose you want to delete the client record for the IPG company, for example:

```
DELETE FROM Clients
WHERE Client_Code = 16
```

When you run this query in MS Access the following message appears:

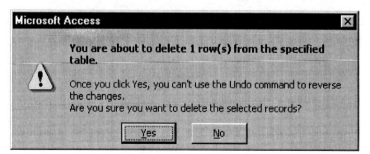

 As a general rule, it is safer to specify the primary key in the **WHERE** clause, to be sure you delete the record you intend to delete.

Introduction

When you create a recordset, you must specify how you want to query your database. The idea is to create SQL queries dynamically, according to the values the user enters or sends, or according to system variables. How you code the data extraction depends on the technique and the server model you choose.

In the **Recordset** dialog box, in simple mode, you can choose the technique you want to use in the third **Filter** pop-up menu:

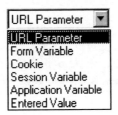

— using a URL parameter,

— using a search form,

— extracting the contents of a cookie,

— extracting the contents of a session variable,

— extracting the contents of an application variable,

— using an entered value.

UltraDev generates all the value extraction scripts, automatically.

In advanced mode, you must program the value extraction yourself, using the language corresponding to your server model.

Name	Default Value	Run-time Value
vCatCode	%	Request.form("Category_Code")

*The above example specifies the extraction of the contents of the "Category_Code"
form into the variable called vCatCode.*

Defining settings in simple mode

*In simple mode, you can use a query with a single condition. UltraDev generates all
the code to create the variable and to extract the conditional value from the SQL
query.*

URL parameters

The user queries the database via a search form using the **GET** *method (sending the
value via the URL). This method passes the conditional value directly to the page
that contains the recordset, via the URL address.*

🔁 Create a search form.

🔁 Give a name to your search form.

🔁 Give a name to your field (use the same name as that of the corresponding
database field).

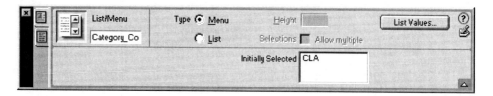

🔁 Open the properties of the form. In the **Method** pop-up menu choose **GET**.
In the **Action** box, enter or select the name of the ASP, JSP or ColdFusion
file that contains the recordset (you must have previously saved your recordset as a file).

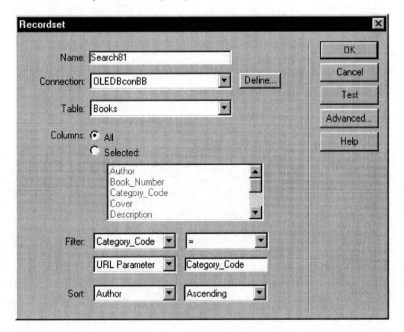

In simple mode, open your ASP, JSP or ColdFusion file that contains the recordset.

Under **Filter** choose the following items:

— the database field you want to query,

— the relational operator,

— the **URL Parameter** option,

— enter the name of the form field that contains the value you need to use as a condition for your SQL query.

In the case where you pass the value via the URL (without a form, in the format: site address/page name?parameter=value),

enter the name of the parameter that contains the value you require in the fourth **Filter** box. For example:

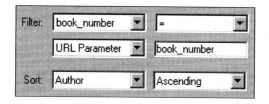

Form variable

*In this case, the user queries the database via a search form, using the **POST** method (sending the value via the http header).*

📁 Create a search form.

📁 Give a name to your search form.

📁 Give a name to your field (use the same name as that of the corresponding database field).

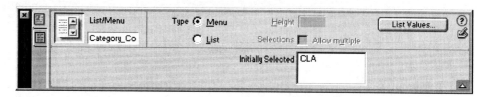

📁 Open the properties of the form. In the **Method** pop-up menu choose **POST**. In the **Action** box, enter or select the name of the ASP, JSP or ColdFusion file that contains the recordset (you must have previously saved your recordset as a file).

| Form Name | Action | Search81.asp |
| CCodeForm | Method | POST |

⊟ In simple mode, open your ASP, JSP or ColdFusion file that contains the recordset.

⊟ Under **Filter** choose the following items:

— the database field you want to query,

— the relational operator,

— the **Form Variable** option,

— enter the name of the form field that contains the value you need to use as a condition for your SQL query.

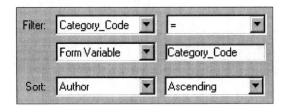

Filter:	Category_Code	▼	=	▼
	Form Variable	▼	Category_Code	
Sort:	Author	▼	Ascending	▼

Cookie

In this case, the server puts a cookie on the user's machine. You must copy the contents of the cookie into a variable, to structure the SQL query.

⊟ You must have previously created a cookie, as follows:

— in **ASP**:

```
Response.Cookies("Identifier") = value
```

— in **JSP**:

```
Cookie identifier = new Cookie ("identifier", value)
Response.addCookie(Identifier)
```

— in **ColdFusion**:

```
<CFCOOKIE name=#Identifier# Value="#value#">
```

 Replace value by the code to get this value. For example, if you create a cookie from the contents of a form field, use the following code:

— in **ASP**:

```
value =Request("Identifier")
```

— in **JSP**:

```
value =request.getParameter("Identifier")
```

— in **ColdFusion**:

```
value =#Identifier#
```

⊡ In simple mode, open your ASP, JSP or ColdFusion file that contains the recordset.

⊡ Under **Filter** choose the following items:

— the database field you want to query,

— the relational operator,

— the **Cookie** option,

— enter the name of the cookie that contains the value you need to use as a condition for your SQL query:

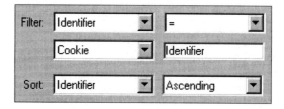

Setting-up queries

Session variable

A session variable allows you to manage information that is specific to each user connected to your site. The system creates the session when the user logs on and deletes it when the user logs off.

You can obtain the contents of the session variable, as a condition for your SQL query.

You must have previously created a session variable, as follows:

— in **ASP**:

```
Session("User") = value
```

— in **JSP**:

```
SessionSetAttribute = ("User", value)
```

— in **ColdFusion**:

```
Session.value
```

 Replace value by the code that will allow you to get this value. For example, if you create a session variable from the contents of a form field, use the following code:

— in **ASP**:

```
value =Request("User")
```

— in **JSP**:

```
value =request.getParameter("User")
```

— in **ColdFusion**:

```
value =#User#
```

In simple mode, open your ASP, JSP or ColdFusion file that contains the recordset.

Under **Filter** choose the following items:

- the database field you want to query,

- the relational operator,

- the **Session Variable** option,

- enter the name of the variable that contains the value you need to use as a condition for your SQL query:

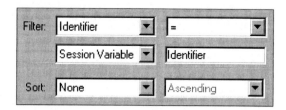

Application variable (ASP and ColdFusion)

An application variable covers all the pages in a site. All the users who connect to your site can use the information that an application variable stores. The ASP file global.asa or the ColdFusion file application.cfm defines the application tasks and settings.

You must create a file that contains your application's settings:

- the **ASP** (VBScript) file **global.asa**:

```
Sub application_OnStart
Code
End Sub
Sub application_OnEnd
Code
End Sub
Sub session_OnStart
Code
End Sub
Sub session_OnEnd
Code
End Sub
```

— the **ColdFusion** file **application.cfm**:

```
<cfapplication name="catalogue"
clientmanagement="Yes"
sessionmanagement="Yes"
setclientcookies="Yes"
sessiontimeout="#CreateTimeSpan(0,1,0,0)#"
applicationtimeout="#CreateTimeSpan(0,0,10,0)#">
```

⊡ In simple mode, open your ASP or ColdFusion file that contains the recordset.

⊡ Under **Filter** choose the following items:

— the database field you want to query,

— the relational operator,

— the **Application Variable** option,

— enter the name of the variable that contains the value you need to use
as a condition for your SQL query:

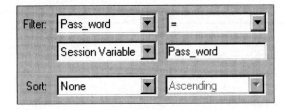

Entered value

*In this case, the search condition of your SQL query is fixed and not a variable
chosen by the session or application user.*

⊡ In simple mode, open your ASP, JSP or ColdFusion file that contains the
SQL query is fixed and not a variable chosen by the session recordset.

⊡ Under **Filter** choose the following items:

— the database field you want to query,

— the relational operator,

— the **Entered Value** option,

— enter the value you need to use as a condition for your SQL query:

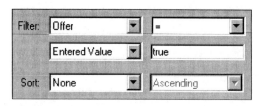

Defining settings in advanced mode

In advanced mode, you can use a query with several conditions. You must write all the scripts to create variables and to get values from a form, a URL parameter, a cookie, a session variable or an application variable. You must also structure your SQL query using the variables you have defined.

Create your variables as follows:

⊟ In advanced mode, open your ASP or ColdFusion file that contains the recordset.

⊟ Under **Variables**, add a new variable by clicking the ➕ button (use the ➖ button to delete a variable).

⊟ Enter a **Name** for your variable.

⊟ Enter a **Default Value** for your variable.

⊟ In the **Run-time Value** column, enter the ASP, JSP or ColdFusion code that determines the content of your variable:

Name	Default Value	Run-time Value
VarCCode	%	Request("Category_Code")
VarAuthor	%	Request("Author")

Under **SQL**, enter your SQL query using the variables you have defined:

```
SELECT *
FROM Books
WHERE Category_Code = 'VarCCode' and Author LIKE 'VarAuthor%'
```

The following example shows settings you can use to create a variable whose value must come from a search form. The user starts the search after entering or selecting a value in the **Category_Code** field of the form.

— in **ASP**:

Name	Default Value	Run-Time Value
VarCCode	%	Request("Category_Code")

— in **JSP**:

Name	Default Value	Run-Time Value
VarCCode	%	Request.getParameter("Category_Code")

— in **ColdFusion**:

Name	Default Value	Run-Time Value
VarCCode	%	#Category_Code#

To use advanced mode you must have a sound knowledge of SQL and of the server technology you are using.

Introduction

A recordset is a data table that contains information you extract from a database. UltraDev displays the recordset field names in the **Data Bindings** window, to allow you to insert them into your results page. To create a results page, you must position your dynamic fields where they must appear in the page then format them using UltraDev's formatting tools. When you run your page on the server, the dynamic field codes are replaced by their contents from the database. The data is formatted according to the field codes, which you can apply either directly or via a CSS style sheet.

 This book uses the terms **fields** or **dynamic data** rather than the term **dynamic text**, which UltraDev often uses.

Your results page will generally show more than one record. You can use repeat regions in order to display all your recordset data.

Inserting dynamic data

⊡ Choose the **Window - Data Bindings** menu option (or simply click the **Data Bindings** tab if the **Server Behaviors** panel is open).

*You can also use the **Data Bindings** button on the **Launcher** bar.*

⊡ Click the ⊞ icon next to **Recordset** to expand your recordset and display its contents.

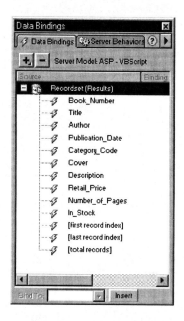

The list of database fields appears.

One after the other, drag each of the fields to the exact place you want it to appear in your page (into a data cell, for example).

Alternatively, you can select your dynamic field, place the insertion point where you want it to appear in the page and click the **Insert** button at the bottom of the **Data Bindings** window.

By default, UltraDev displays the dynamic field codes and not the field contents, in the format: {recordset.fieldname}, for example: {Results.Category_Code}, where Results is the recordset name and Category_Code is the database field name.

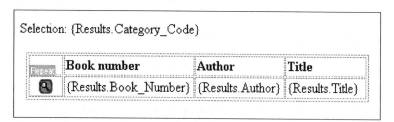

You can format each of your dynamic fields (to specify its font, size, colour and so forth) or you can use CSS styles.

To work directly on the recordset data, switch to **Live Data** mode (see the **Testing your dynamic pages** chapter).

You can choose how you want your dynamic data to appear. For this purpose, select the **Edit - Preferences** menu option. Select the **Invisible Elements** category and choose to **Show Dynamic Test As** either **{Recordset.Field}** or **{}**.

Formatting dynamic data

*You can format dynamic data directly using the **Data Bindings** window. For example, you can choose to display a price with two decimal places or change the format of a date. UltraDev offers a different set according to the **server model** you are using.*

 To apply a format, select the field you want to format in the page and choose from the pop-up menu in the **Format** column of the **Data Bindings** window.

Here are the formats UltraDev provides with ASP:

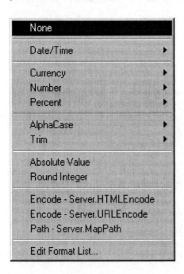

Here are the formats UltraDev provides with JSP:

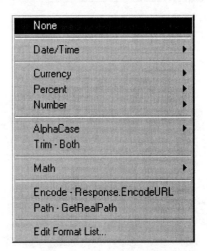

Here are the formats UltraDev provides with ColdFusion:

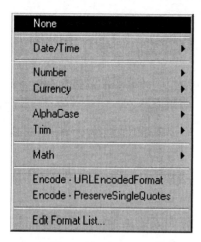

 To apply some of these formats, you need a sound knowledge of ASP, JSP or ColdFusion technology.

Modifying a format

⊡ Select a dynamic field and open the pop-up menu in the **Format** column of the **Data Bindings** window.

⊡ Choose the **Edit Format List** option.

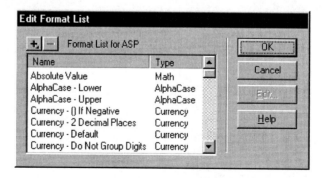

⊡ Double-click the format you want to edit then indicate the modifications to make to this format:

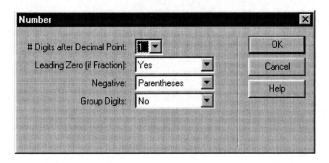

⊡ Click **OK**.

 Some formats cannot be modified.

Creating a new format

⊡ Select a dynamic field and open the pop-up menu in the **Format** column of the **Data Bindings** window.

⊡ Choose the **Edit Format List** option.

⊡ Click the ⊞ button to add a new format.

⊡ Choose the **Type** of your new format.

⊡ Specify your format.

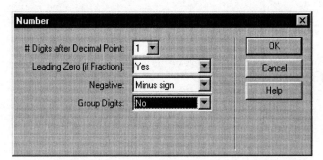

Click **OK**.

 Enter a **Name** for your new format.

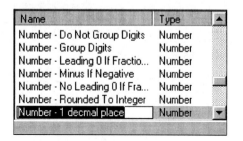

If you choose to **Get More Formats** when you click the button in the **Edit Format List** dialog box, UltraDev connects you to the Macromedia site to allow you to download other formats.

Creating a dynamic image

You can display an image dynamically from its file (image.gif or image.jpg) in the database. For example, in the case of a product catalogue you can display a description of a product along with its photo. If you are using Microsoft Access you must create a text field and enter the name of the image file for the product.

UltraDev does not support BLOBs (Binary Large OBjects) in databases.

 **Insert
Image**

 In the **Select File Name From** frame, choose the **Data Sources** option.

 If necessary, expand your recordset and select the field that contains the database image files.

You do not need to apply a format in this case.

↪ In the **URL** box, UltraDev displays the ASP, JSP or ColdFusion code for the field.

— with **ASP**: <%=(recordset.Fields.Item("fieldname").Value)%>

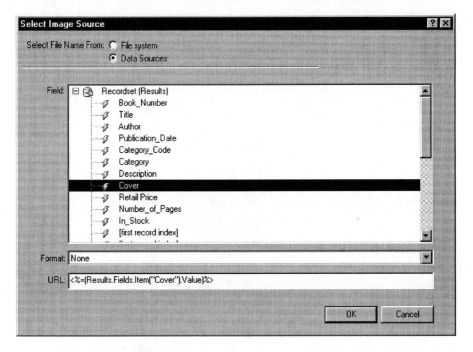

UltraDev inserts the icon to symbolise a dynamic image object.

> 💡 It is better to store only the file name in the database, rather than the full access path. It is easier to indicate the full access path in the **URL** box. This approach accommodates any modifications you may make to your site's file hierarchy. For example, if the folder db/covers contains the image files, with ASP the URL is as follows:
> dB/covers/<%=(Results.Fields.Item("cover").Value)%>
> Images access path <%fieldcode%>

Creating a repeat region

A repeat region allows you to display all the recordset information in the results page (otherwise you will display only the first record).
You can indicate whether your results page must send all the recordset information or only a limited number of records per page. If you limit the number of records per page, you must insert a navigation bar to consult the data page by page.

Select the dynamic data you want to repeat. In the **Server Behaviors** window, click the 🔳 button and choose **Repeat Region**.

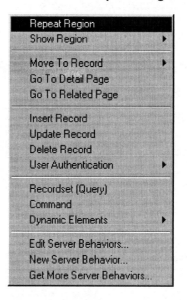

Select your **Recordset** from the pop-up menu.

Choose to **Show** either **All Records** or a specific number of records per page (10 by default).

Creating results pages
125

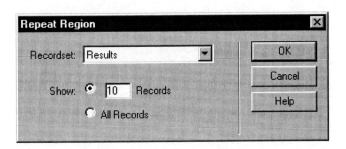

Showing and hiding a region

The **Show Region** behavior allows you to specify the conditions for showing or hiding information on a page. For example, you may wish to hide your results table if it does not contain any records or you may want to display **No records found** when the recordset is empty.

In the **Server Behaviors** window, click the button and choose **Show Region** and select the rule you want to apply:

In the following example, if the recordset is not empty, the results page shows the total number of records and a results table with three dynamic fields. If the recordset is empty it displays the text **No records found!**

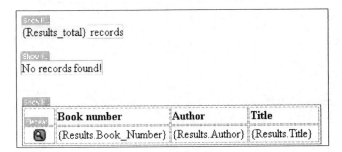

Displaying record statistics

UltraDev provides three standard dynamic fields for creating record counters:

— first record index,

— last record index,

— total records.

For example, if your recordset contains 30 records, the total records will be 30, the first record index will be 1 and the last record index will be 30. If your page displays the recordset data in groups of 10 records (in a repeat region) the first record index will be 1 and the last record index will be 10.

To implement a record counter, open the **Data Bindings** window.

Drag each of the [first record index], [last record index] and [total records] fields onto the page (or for each field in turn, position the insertion point in the page then select the field in the **Data Bindings** window and click the **Insert** button).

Record {Results_first} of {Results_total}

Records {Results_first} to {Results_last} of {Results_total}

For example, if you display a page that contains 628 records in the **Live Data** *window you will view one of the following texts:*

- *Record 1 of 628,*

- *Records 1 to 10 of 628 (in the case of a repeat region that returns the records by groups of 10).*

Creating navigation links

*UltraDev provides two methods for creating navigation links in a recordset: you can use the **Recordset Navigation Bar** (see the **Live objects** chapter) or you can create your own navigation bar element by element (see below):*

If you want to create a specific navigation link, select the text corresponding to your link ("Next record", for example) or if you want to create an image link, select the image concerned.

By default, UltraDev creates the following text links:

— First

— Previous

— Next

— Last.

In the **Server Behaviors** window, click the  button, select **Move To Record** and choose the navigation element you want to insert in the page.

> Move To First Record
> Move To Previous Record
> Move To Next Record
> Move To Last Record
> Move To Specific Record

Here is an example of a **Move To Next Record** text link:

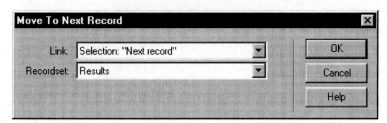

Here is an example of a **Move To Next Record** image link:

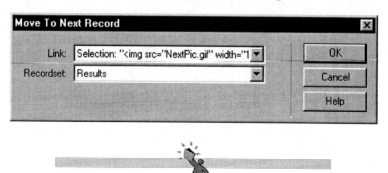

The Live Data environment

The UltraDev **Live Data** window allows you to display the results of your dynamic pages. You can position and format your dynamic data directly in the page. Furthermore, you can set up the Live Data environment to test all your queries and view your page setup for any set of data.

According to your recordset, this technique allows you to change the column width and row height of a results table and to choose a format (font, size, colour and so forth).

Dreamweaver uses your Web server to run your dynamic pages in Live Data mode (by creating a temporary file that runs on your server).

To use this mode, you must have defined the **URL Prefix** setting (see the **Defining a site** chapter).

Switching to Live Data mode

↵ **View**
Live Data

Ctrl Shift **R** (PC)
⌘ Shift **R** (Mac)

An additional bar appears under the UltraDev menus.

Refreshing Live Data

You can refresh your live data either automatically or manually.

↵ **View**
Refresh Live Data

Ctrl **R** (PC)
⌘ **R** (Mac)

↵ If you want UltraDev to refresh your live data automatically, activate the **Auto refresh** check box on the toolbar.

Defining Live Data settings

UltraDev allows you to simulate the execution of your queries using different conditions and to check your data formatting.

☐ **View**
  Live Data Settings

☐ Under **URL Request** click the  button then enter the **Name** of your variable (use the same name as you used in the recordset) and the test **Value** you want to assign to your variable.

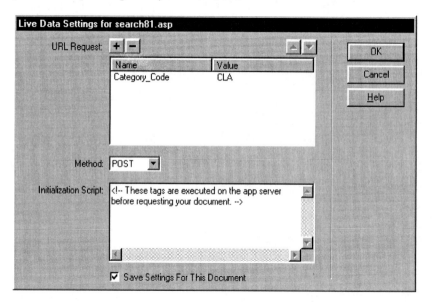

☐ In the **Method** pop-up menu, choose how you want to transmit the form data (either **GET** or **POST**) that you defined when you created your recordset.

In the **Initialization Script** box, enter the statements that the server must run before loading the page. For example, when a user connects to your books catalogue, providing an identifier and a password, you need to get your client's Member or Non-member status in a session variable (as members benefit from special rates). Enter your **Initialization Script**, according to the server model you are using:

— in **ASP**:

```
<% session("MM_UserAuthorization")="Member" %>
```

— in **JSP**:

```
<% session.put.value("MM_UserAuthorization", "Member") %>
```

— In **Coldfusion**:

```
<CFSET session. "MM_UserAuthorization"="Member">
```

 If you activate the **Save Settings For This Document** check box, UltraDev will save all your successive Live Date settings in the **Design Notes** dialog box (**File - Design Notes**).

Links do not operate in the **Live Data** window.

Previewing in your browser

*You can view your pages using the **Preview in Browser** command. UltraDev runs your pages on the application server.*

File
Preview in Browser
Edit Browser List

Activate the **Preview Using Application Server** check box.

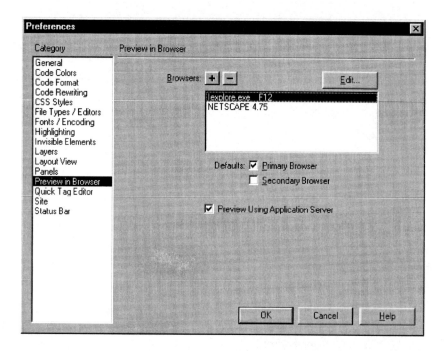

Testing in your browser

 Start your Web browser and enter the URL of your site in the address bar.

For example, if you created your site pages in the C:\inetpub\wwwroot\catalogue folder, you can test your site on your Web server by entering the URL in one of the following ways:

— http://computer_name/catalogue

— http://localhost/catalogue

— http://127.0.0.1/catalogue

To test your ASP pages, you need start your Web server only. To test your JSP or ColdFusion pages, you must start your Web server and your application server (your JRun or your ColdFusion server, for example).

Introduction

UltraDev offers a set of server behaviors that allow you to manage the access to your Internet site. You can implement:

— a registration form in which the user must enter information such as his/her name (identifier or login name) and password, the database stores the transmitted data,

— a behavior that checks if the username already exists in the database (to avoid duplicates),

— a site access form for visitors who have already registered,

— a behavior to manage access restrictions to specific pages on your site.

Creating a registration form

Insert in your page a form containing at least two text fields: one for the username and one for the password:

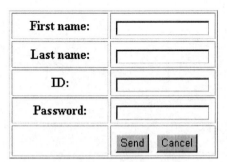

In the property inspector, give a name to your form and to each of the fields.

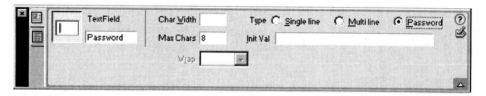

⤵ In the **Server Behaviors** window, click the ➕ button then choose the **Insert Record** option.

⤵ Select the **Connection** from the corresponding pop-up menu, which contains all the connections your have defined for the site.

⤵ Using the **Insert Into Table** pop-up menu, choose the table in which you want to store the user's data.

⤵ In the **After Inserting, Go To** box, enter the name of the file you want the user to view after registration, or click the **Browse** button to select it.

⤵ Select the name of your form in the **Get Values From** pop-up menu.

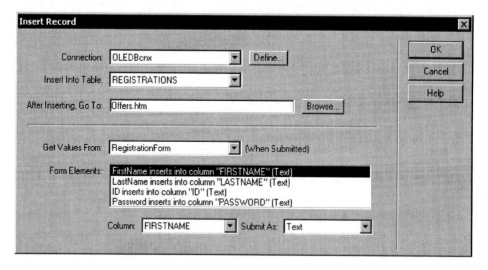

⤵ In the **Form Elements** box, associate your form field names with your database field names. If your form field names are the same as the database field names, UltraDev will associate these names automatically.

*You must use the following template for this purpose: **your_form_field_name inserts into column"database_field_name"(database_field-type)**.*

To modify an association, in the **Form Elements** box, select the line you want to modify then, choose from the **Column** pop-up menu, the name of the database field that must receive the data.

Using the **Submit As** pop-up menu, choose the format for this data:

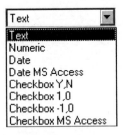

Click **OK** to confirm your insertion.

Checking the username

In the **Server Behaviors** window, click the [+] button then choose the **User Authentication** option followed by the **Check New Username** option.

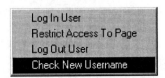

Using the **Username Field** pop-up menu, choose the field name. The field must not contain duplicates.

In the **If Already Exists, Go To** box, enter the name of the file you want the user to view in this case, or click the **Browse** button to select it.

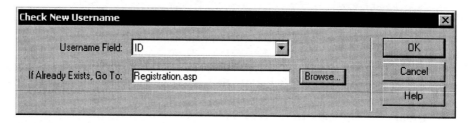

Click **OK**.

Logging in a user

You must have previously created a form containing at least two text fields: one for the username and one for the password. You will not authorize access to your Web site unless your database contains the username and password.

Make sure you have named your form and your form fields.

In the **Server Behaviors** window, click the ⊞ button then choose the **User Authentication** option followed by the **Log In User** option.

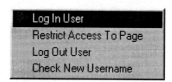

*The **Log In User** dialog box contains four frames in which you must specify the following information:*

- *information concerning your form,*

- *information concerning your database,*

- *forwarding instructions in case of success or failure,*

- *access restrictions.*

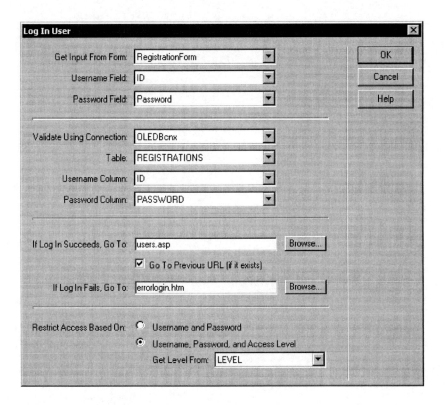

Information concerning your form

⊡ **Get Input From Form**: choose the name of your form.

⊡ **Username Field**: choose the corresponding form field.

⊡ **Password Field**: choose the corresponding form field.

Information concerning your database

⊡ **Validate Using Connection**: choose the name of your database connection.

⊡ **Table**: choose the table in which the **Username** and the **Password** must be checked.

⊡ **Username Column**: choose the corresponding database field.

⊡ **Password Column**: choose the corresponding database field.

Forwarding instructions in case of success or failure

⊡ **If Log In Succeeds, Go To**: enter the corresponding filename, or click the **Browse** button to select it.

⊡ **If Log In Fails, Go To**: enter the corresponding filename, or click the **Browse** button to select it.

Access restrictions

Authentication is carried out on the username, the password and a database field that contains a privilege level.

⊡ **Restrict Access Based On**: choose one of the following options:

Username and Password The username and password are checked: if the database contains this data, the user is allowed to view the **If Log In Succeeds** file.

Username, Password, and Access Level: use the **Get Level From** pop-up menu to choose the database field that contains the user access privileges.

At this point, you need indicate only that you want to test the users access privilege level (as well as the username and password).

To implement a second level of access control on a specific page, you must specify the **Restrict Access To Page** server behavior in that page (see below).

Restricting access to a page

The Restrict Access To Page behavior allows a user to access a page after you have checked the username and password. In addition, you can check whether the user has the required privilege level to view a restricted access page. The database contains the user's access level, which must correspond to the level you have defined in the page.

⊟ In the **Server Behaviors** window, click the ⊞ button then choose the **User Authentication** option followed by the **Restrict Access To Page** option.

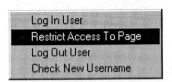

⊟ Choose a **Restrict Based On** option: **Username and Password** or **Username, Password, and Access Level**.

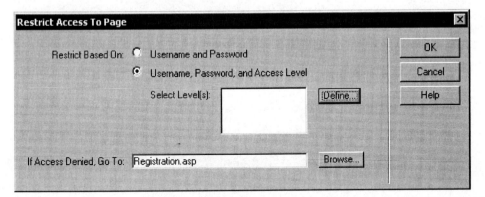

⊟ If you choose the **Username, Password, and Access Level** option, click the **Define** button to specify your access level(s):

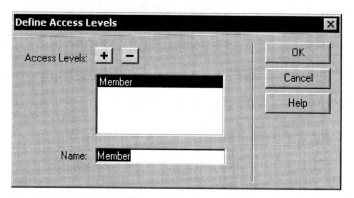

⊟ Enter the **Name** of your level and click the ⊞ button. To select several access levels, use the ⌈Ctrl⌋ key (PC) or the ⌈⌘⌋ key (Mac).

⊟ Click **OK** twice.

Introduction

Suppose a user carries out a search on your site and views a results page, where all the records that meet his/her search conditions appear.

For the user to be able to display further information on a specific record in the list, you must have created a detail page. A detail page displays one record only.

UltraDev allows you to link your master page containing several records to the detail page containing the record requested on the master page.

The selection condition is sent from the master page to the detail page via a URL in the following format:
http://site_address/detail_page_name?condition=value

Creating the master page

Your master page must contain a recordset to which you must add a link to the detail page.

⊟ Place the insertion point where you want to create the link or select the image you want to use for your link.

⊟ In the **Server Behaviors** window, click the ⊞ button then choose the **Go To Detail Page** option.

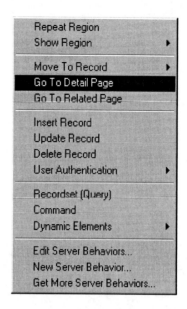

In the **Link** pop-up menu, choose the link code (either for a text link or for an image link if you selected an image).

Text link

Image link

In the **Detail Page** box, enter the name of your detail page file, or click the **Browse** button to select it.

In the **Pass URL Parameter** box, enter the name of the database field whose value you want to send to the detail page, via the URL.

Using the **Recordset** and **Column** pop-up menus, select the names of the recordset and the field that contain the URL parameter value.

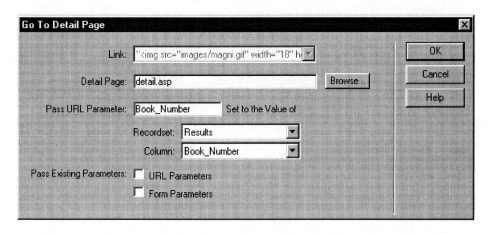

🔁 If you want to pass existing **URL Parameters** or **Form Parameters** in this page, activate the corresponding check box.

For example, a user may search for "Classics" books in a catalogue. When the user clicks a specific book to see the detail page, in addition to the book reference number, you pass the existing category parameter in the page (Category_Code=CLA).

Creating the detail page

You must add a recordset to indicate that the detail page will receive a selection condition via a URL parameter.

🔁 In the **Server Behaviors** window, click the ➕ button then choose the **Recordset (Query)** option.

🔁 Enter a **Name** for your recordset and select your database **Connection**.

🔁 Under **Filter**, set up your SQL query as follows:

Database field name   =

URL Parameter   name of URL parameter

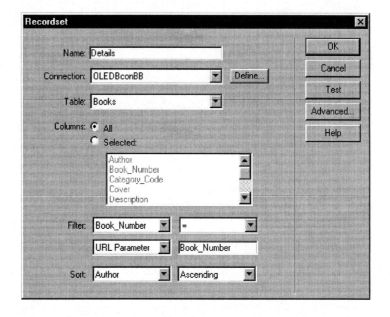

 It is preferable to use a unique database field as your selection condition (either a primary key or a unique identifier). This value will be sent via the URL.

➕ Insert and format your dynamic fields in the detail page.

➕ Here is an example of a detail page:

Reference number:	{Details.Book_Number}
Author:	{Details.Author}
Title:	{Details.Title}
Publication date:	{Details.Publication_Date}
Our price:	{Details.Retail_Price}

In the following example, the master page passes to the detail page (details.asp) the number of the required database record:

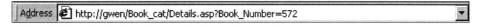

Introduction

Related pages allow you to pass parameters from one page to another. You pass your parameters by adding to the page's URL, the name and value of the parameter, in the following format:
http://www.mysite.com/index2.asp?Lastname=Jenkins
With this approach, you need extract only your URL parameters.

Creating a related page

🔁 Select the text or the image you want to use as a link to your related page.

🔁 In the **Server Behaviors** window, click the ➕ button then choose the **Go To Related Page** option.

🔁 Choose your link from the **Link** pop-up menu. UltraDev displays the link code that corresponds to the image you selected (Selection: "<text or image link code>": if you did not select a text or image, UltraDev creates a default link with the text **Related**).

🔁 In the **Related Page** field, enter the name of the related page, or click the **Browse** button to select it.

🔁 Choose how you want to **Pass Existing Parameters** to the related page: select

URL Parameters   if you will obtain the parameters from a form using the GET method,

Form Parameters   if you will obtain the parameters from a form using the POST method.

Related pages

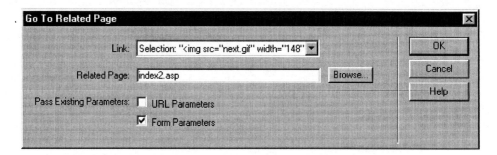

For example, if you receive a user's first and last name via a form and you want to send them to a related page, you must activate the **Form Parameters** check box to allow UltraDev to pass this information via the URL:

⊡ Click **OK**.

Getting parameters

*To get a parameter, you must create a **Request Variable** in the **Data Bindings** window.*

⊡ Open the **Data Bindings** window.

For ASP

⊡ Click the ⊞ button then choose the **Request Variable** option.

⊡ Select **Request** from the **Type** pop-up menu.

⊡ Enter a **Name** for your parameter.

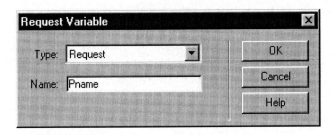

⊡ Click **OK**.

*The parameter is available in the **Request** object and you can drag it onto your page.*

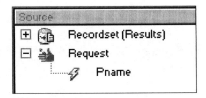

For JSP

⊡ Click the 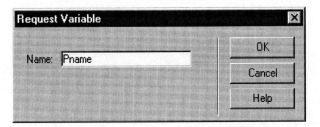 button then choose the **Request Variable** option.

⊡ Enter a **Name** for your parameter.

⊡ Click **OK**.

*The parameter is available in the **Request** object and you can drag it onto your page.*

For ColdFusion

⊡ Click the 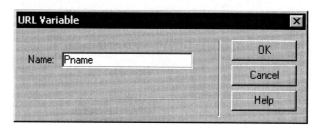 button then choose the **URL Variable** option.

⊡ Enter a **Name** for your parameter.

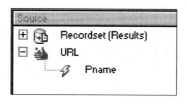

⊡ Click **OK**.

> The parameter is available in the **Request** object and you can drag it onto your page.

Introduction

UltraDev offers a set of live objects to help you create the following items in one operation:

— a detail page linked to a master page,

— a navigation bar and counter for a recordset,

— a form for inserting or updating information in a database.

Creating a master-detail page set

A master page generally displays the main fields of a recordset. Each record in the master page can contain a link that allows the user to view additional information on a selected record on a detail page.

First, you must create a master page and define a recordset.

⤵ Select **File - New** then save your file in ASP, JSP or ColdFusion.

⤵ Add a recordset to your page and set it up.

⤵ Insert a live object:

Insert
Live Objects
Master Detail Page Set

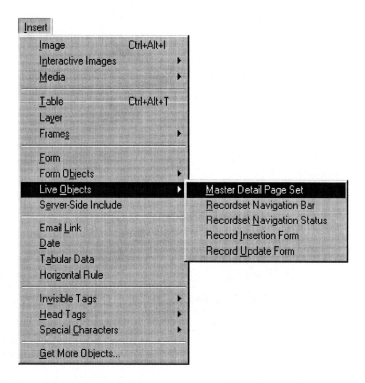

*The **Insert Master-Detail Page Set** dialog box contains all the parameters for master and detail pages.*

⊡ Select the **Recordset** you want to use.

⊡ The **Master Page Fields** pane lists the recordset fields: you can add fields using the [+] button and delete fields using the [−] button.

⊡ You can change the order of the fields by moving them upwards (⬆) or downwards (⬇).

*Be careful: UltraDev will create a results table in the page using these **Master Page Fields** in the order you define.*

☐ Using the **Link To Detail From** pop-up menu, choose the field name you want to use for the link to the detail page.

☐ Using the **Pass Unique Key** pop-up menu, choose the name of the field whose value you want to send to the detail page (it is generally better to choose the primary key for this purpose, as its values are unique).

☐ Choose whether you want to **Show** a specific number of **Records at a Time** (10 by default) or whether you want to show **All Records**.

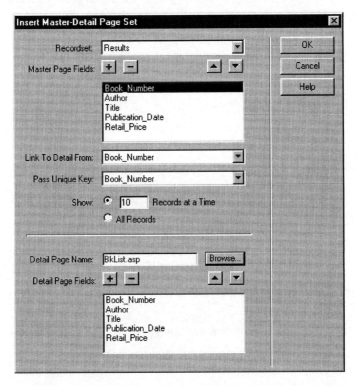

☐ Enter the **Detail Page Name** or click the **Browse** button to select this file. If the file does not exist, UltraDev will create it automatically.

⊟ Choose the **Detail Page Fields**: you can delete fields using the ⊟ button and add (deleted) fields using the ⊕ button. You can change the order of the fields by moving them upwards (▲) or downwards (▼). UltraDev will use this order when it inserts the information in the detail page.

⊟ Click **OK**.

UltraDev creates the results table in the detail page:

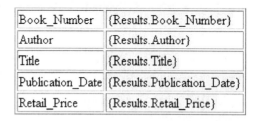

Book_Number	{Results.Book_Number}
Author	{Results.Author}
Title	{Results.Title}
Publication_Date	{Results.Publication_Date}
Retail_Price	{Results.Retail_Price}

UltraDev creates the recordset automatically along with the URL parameters that must be passed between the master page and the detail pages:

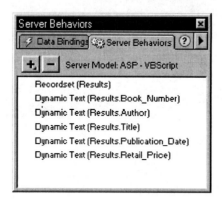

*UltraDev creates the results table in the master page along with a recordset naviga-
tion bar and a record counter (for example **Records 1 to 10 of 120**). In addition,
UltraDev implements the hyperlink on the specified field to open the detail page:*

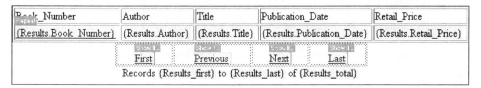

Book_Number	Author	Title	Publication_Date	Retail_Price
{Results.Book_Number}	{Results.Author}	{Results.Title}	{Results.Publication_Date}	{Results.Retail_Price}

First   Previous   Next   Last

Records {Results_first} to {Results_last} of {Results_total}

UltraDev adds the **Go To Detail Page** server behavior and the other server
behaviors that allow you to manage the recordset navigation bar.

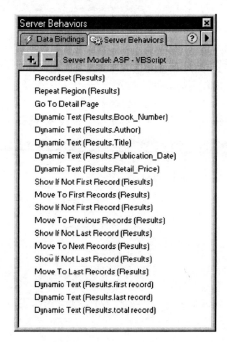

Creating a recordset navigation bar

You can create a navigation system for a recordset. UltraDev automatically sets up the behaviors to allow you to move to the first, last, previous or next records.

↪ You must have previously added a recordset to the page.

↪ **Insert**
Live Objects
Recordset Navigation Bar

↪ Choose a **Recordset**.

↪ Choose a **Text** or **Images** display for your recordset navigation bar.

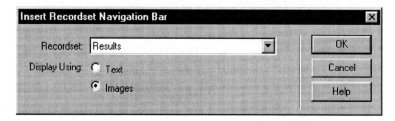

↪ Click **OK**.

*If you choose the **Images** option, UltraDev inserts the first.gif, previous.gif, next.gif and last.gif images into the bar.*

Text navigation bar:

Images navigation bar:

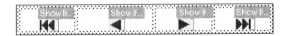

If there is no "next record" or "previous record" in your recordset, UltraDev hides the next button or the previous button. UltraDev automatically adds the behaviors required to manage the recordset navigation bar:

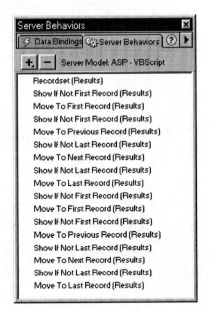

Creating a record insertion form

UltraDev allows you to generate a form to insert data into a database.

⊟ **Insert**
   Live Objects
   Record Insertion Form

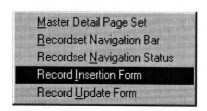

Master Detail Page Set
Recordset Navigation Bar
Recordset Navigation Status
Record Insertion Form
Record Update Form

⊟ Choose your database **Connection**. If have not yet set up a database connection, click the **Define** button to create one.

⊟ From the **Insert Into Table** pop-up menu, choose the table into which you want to add records.

⊟ In the **After Inserting, Go To** box enter the name of the page you want to display after inserting data, or click the **Browse** button to select it.

⊟ The **Form Fields** box lists the recordset fields: you can add fields using the ⊞ button and delete fields using the ⊟ button. You can change the order of the fields by moving them upwards (▲) or downwards (▼).

⊟ You can modify the **Label** of each of these fields (by default, UltraDev uses the names of the database fields). The **Label** will appear next to the form field.

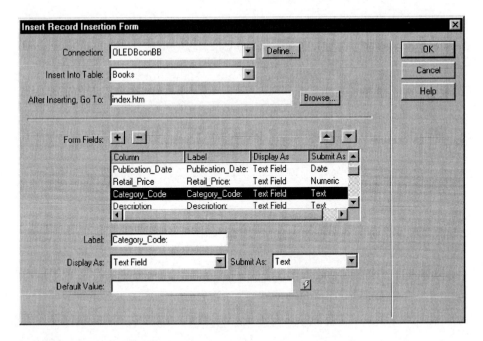

☐ From the **Display As** pop-up menu, choose the field type for each of the form fields you want to create:

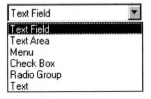

☐ From the **Submit As** pop-up menu, choose the format for the data you want to submit to the database via the form:

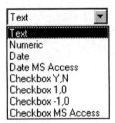

⊡ You can specify a **Default Value** for each of your form fields.

    — For a **Text Field**, you can either enter a value or insert a value from the database by clicking the **Dynamic Data** button ().

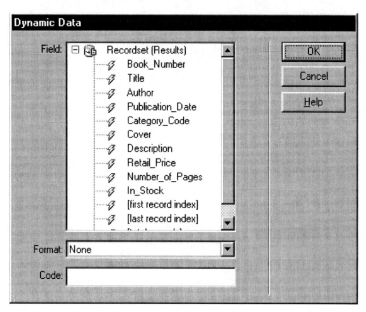

    — For a **Check Box**, you can define the **Initial State**:

    — For a **Radio Group**, you can define the **Radio Group Properties** by clicking the **Radio Group Properties** button.

Choose how you want to create the radio group. If you choose to create the radio group **Manually** you must choose a **Label** and a **Value** for each button in your radio group.

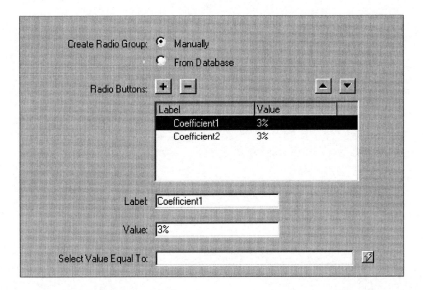

If you choose to create the radio group **From Database** you must choose the **Recordset** you want to use (you must have already created a recordset to use this option).

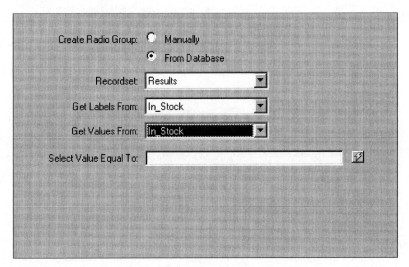

Using the **Get Labels From** and **Get Values From** pop-up menus, choose the database fields whose labels and values you want to use for your radio group.

— For a **Menu**, click the **Menu Properties** button.

The **Menu Properties** set up dialog box and method are similar to those of the **Radio Group Properties** : you choose to create your menu **Manually** by specifying the different menu items or **From Database**, in which case you must have already created a recordset.

If you want to use a menu that shows each field value only once, without duplicates, you must create in your recordset, an SQL **SELECT** statement with the **DISTINCT** clause.

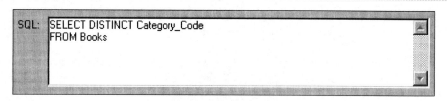

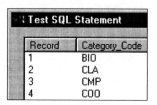

If you want to create dynamic form fields, you must add a recordset to your page (make sure you define your SQL queries correctly).

 When you have finished setting up your **Record Insertion Form**, click the **OK** button.

UltraDev generates the form in the page.

The **Server Behaviors** *window shows the behaviors that UltraDev has added to the page. UltraDev systematically adds the* **Insert Record** *behavior in this case.*

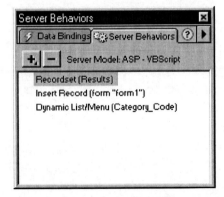

Creating a record update form

The record update object allows you to create a form rapidly, to update fields in a database record.

To use this feature, you must have created a recordset. It is best to consider the record update form as a detail page and to link it to a master page using the **Go To Detail Page** behavior.

When you click a specific record on the master page, you open the form, which allows you to update this record.

⊡ You can insert the record update object as follows:

⊡ **Insert**
Live Objects
Record Update Form

> Master Detail Page Set
> Recordset Navigation Bar
> Recordset Navigation Status
> Record Insertion Form
> Record Update Form

⊡ Choose your database **Connection**. If have not yet set up a database connection, click the **Define** button to create one.

⊡ From the **Table to Update** pop-up menu, choose the table you want to update.

⊡ Using the **Select Records From** pop-up menu, select the recordset that contains the data you want to update. This recordset may be filtered (to update a specific selection of records) or not (to update all the data in the table).

⊡ In the **After Updating, Go To** box enter the name of the page you want to display after updating, or click the **Browse** button to select it.

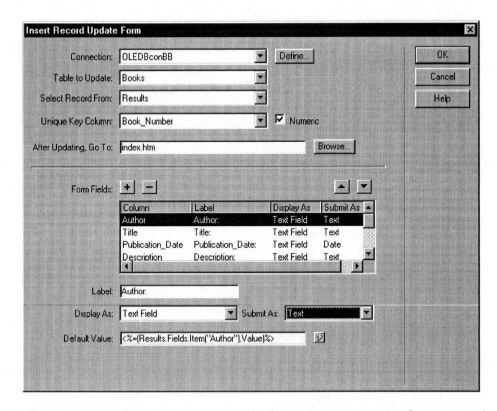

*In the **Form Fields** frame, you must specify the settings you require for creating the update form.*

- Add and delete fields as required (if you use an AutoNumber field as primary key in your access table, for example, this field must not appear in your form).

- You can change the order of the fields by moving them upwards (⬆) or downwards (⬇).

- You can modify the **Label** of each of these fields.

- From the **Display As** pop-up menu, choose a type of object to represent each of the form fields you want to create.

□ From the **Submit As** pop-up menu, choose the format for the data you want to submit to the database via the form (you can choose **Text, Numeric** or **Date** formats, for example).

□ UltraDev supplies the contents of the **Default Value** field, which returns the current contents of each of the record fields before receiving the new value and updating the database.

□ Click **OK**.

UltraDev generates the form in the page and adds the required behaviors to the ***Server Behaviors*** *window.*

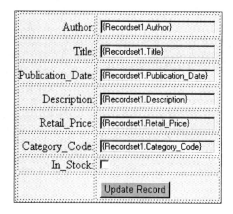

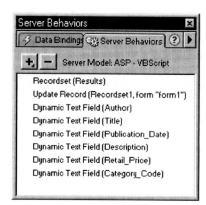

Inserting a record counter

□ Insert
Live Objects
Recordset Navigation Status

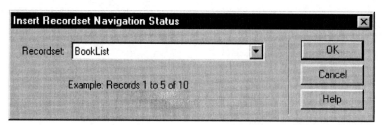

▣ Choose your **Recordset** and click **OK**.

UltraDev inserts the indices for the first record, the last record and the total number of records.

Records {BookList_first} to {BookList_last} of {BookList_total}

Introduction

UltraDev provides three server behaviors to allow you to:

— insert a new record in a database,

— update a record in a database,

— delete a record in a database.

Inserting a record

Create a form containing only the database fields you need. <u>Give a name to your form and to each of the fields</u>. It is generally more convenient to use the same names in the form, as in the database.

 If the database automatically renumbers each new record, do not include an AutoNumber field in your form.

In the **Server Behavior** window, click the ![icon] button and choose **Insert Record**.

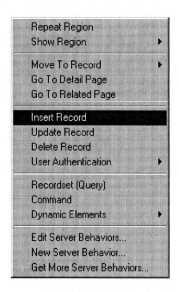

If you have not yet created a form, UltraDev warns you that you must create one before inserting a record:

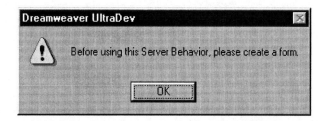

When you have created your form, you can set up the data submission.

□ Choose your database **Connection** or click the **Define** button to create one. Using the **Insert Into Table** pop-up menu, choose the table into which you want to insert the record.

□ In the **After Inserting, Go To** box enter the name of the page you want to view after inserting a record, or click the **Browse** button to select it.

□ In the **Get Values From** pop-up menu, choose your insertion form.

Insert Record ☒

Connection:	OLEDBconBB ▼ Define...
Insert Into Table:	Books ▼
After Inserting, Go To:	index.htm Browse...

OK
Cancel
Help

Get Values From: InsertionForm ▼ (When Submitted)

Form Elements:
Title inserts into column "Title" (Text)
Author inserts into column "Author" (Text)
Category_Code inserts into column "Category_Code" (Text)
In_Stock inserts into column "In_Stock" (Checkbox MS Access)

Column: In_Stock ▼   Submit As: Checkbox MS Acce: ▼

The **Form Elements** pane associates your form field names with your database field names. If your form field names are the same as the database field names, Ultra-Dev will automatically indicate for each of your form fields, the table column (database field) that must receive the data along with the data type (for example, text, numeric, date or checkbox).

⊡ To modify an association, in the **Form Elements** frame, select the line you want to modify then choose from the **Column** pop-up menu, the name of the database field that must receive the data.

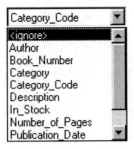

Category_Code ▼

<ignore>
Author
Book_Number
Category
Category_Code
Description
In_Stock
Number_of_Pages
Publication_Date

⊡ To change the submission format of a form field, select the form field in the **Form Elements** frame then choose the format for this data from the **Submit As** pop-up menu.

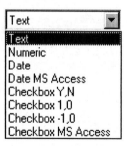

Click **OK**.

UltraDev adds to the form, the `<%=MM_editAction%>` **Action** *for ASP or JSP, or the* `<cfoutput>#MM_editAction</cfoutput>` **Action** *for ColdFusion. UltraDev also adds the* **Insert Record** *action in the* **Server Behaviors** *window.*

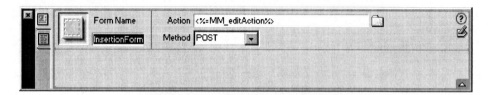

Updating a record

To use this behavior, your page must contain a recordset that defines the data UltraDev can update and a form that allows you to modify some or all the information in a record.

If you have not yet created a recordset or a form, UltraDev warns you that you must create these items before updating a record:

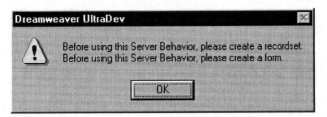

⊟ Create a recordset.

⊟ Create a form containing only the database fields you need. <u>Give a name to your form and to each of the fields</u>. It is generally more convenient to use the same names in the form and in the database.

⊟ In the **Server Behavior** window, click the ⊞ button and choose **Update Record**.

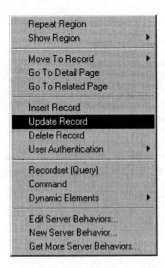

▱ Choose your database **Connection** or click the **Define** button to create one. Choose your **Table to Update**.

▱ Using the **Select Record From** pop-up menu, choose the recordset you want to use as a data source.

▱ Using the **Unique Key Column** pop-up menu, choose the primary key field in the database table.

▱ In the **After Updating, Go To** box enter the name of the page you want to view after updating a record, or click the **Browse** button to select it.

▱ In the **Get Values From** pop-up menu, choose your update form.

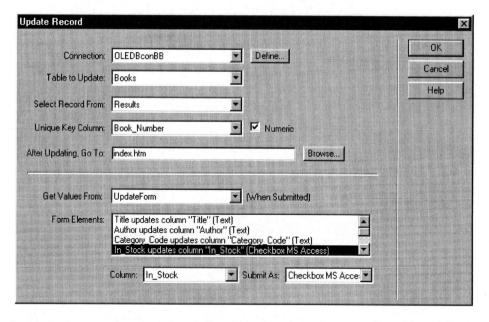

The **Form Elements** pane associates your form field names with your database field names. If your form field names are the same as the database field names, Ultra-Dev will automatically indicate for each of your form fields, the table column (database field) that must receive the data along with the data type (for example, text, numeric, date or checkbox).

To modify an association, select the line you want to modify in the **Form Elements** frame then choose, from the **Column** pop-up menu, the name of the database field that is going to receive the datas.

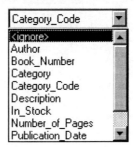

To change the submission format of a form field, select the form field in the **Form Elements** frame then choose the format for this data from the **Submit As** pop-up menu.

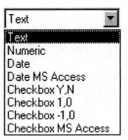

Click **OK**.

UltraDev adds the `<%=MM_editAction%>` ***Action** for ASP or JSP, or the* `<cfoutput>` *#MM_editAction</cfoutput>* ***Action** for ColdFusion. UltraDev also adds the* ***Update Record** action in the **Server Behaviors** window.*

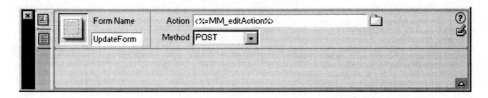

Deleting a record

To use this behavior, your page must contain a recordset that defines the data UltraDev can delete and a form that allows you to select the data to delete.

If you have not yet created a recordset or a form, UltraDev warns you that you must create these items before proceeding:

- Create a recordset.

- Create a form containing only the database fields you need. <u>Give a name to your form and to each of the fields</u>. It is generally more convenient to use the same names in the form and in the database.

- In the **Server Behavior** window, click the button and choose **Delete Record**.

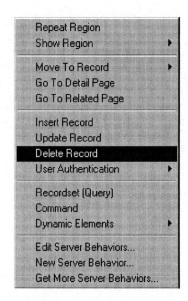

- Choose your database **Connection** or click the **Define** button to create one. Choose the table in which you want to delete data using the **Delete From Table** pop-up menu.

- Using the **Select Record From** pop-up menu, choose the recordset you want to use as a data source.

- Using the **Unique Key Column** pop-up menu, choose the primary key field in the database table.

- In the **After Deleting, Go To** box, enter the name of the page you want to view after deletion, or click the **Browse** button to select it.

- In the **Delete By Submitting** pop-up menu, choose the form you want to use to delete the record.

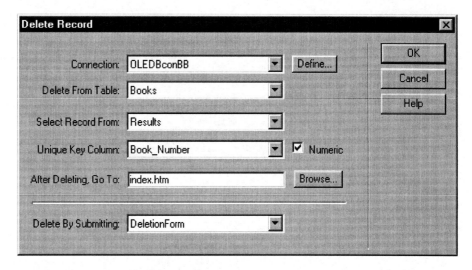

➥ Click **OK** to confirm your insertion.

UltraDev adds the to the form the `<%=MM_editAction%>` ***Action** for ASP or JSP, or the* `<cfoutput>#MM_editAction/<cfoutput>` ***Action** for ColdFusion. UltraDev also adds the **Delete Record** action in the **Server Behaviors** window.*

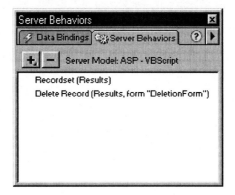

Using live objects

You can implement record insertion or update procedures using **Live Objects** (see the **Live objects** chapter).

With this approach, you can set up your procedures in a single operation and UltraDev automatically generates the corresponding forms.

Prepared (Insert, Update, Delete) behavior in JSP

*The JSP **Prepared** server behavior allows you to create queries to insert, update and delete data. Unlike the **Insert Record**, the **Update Record** and the **Delete Record** server behaviors, the JSP **Prepared** server behavior uses the **JSP PreparedStatement** object. UltraDev pre-compiles the SQL query before it runs it on the database. This approach enhances the performance of your application.*

⊡ In the **Server Behavior** window, click the 🔲 button and choose **Prepared (Insert,Update,Delete)**.

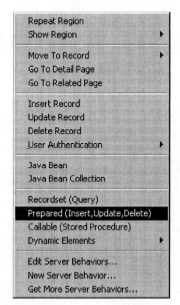

⊡ Enter the **Name** of your procedure and choose your database **Connection**.

Using the **Type** pop-up menu, choose the type of query you want to run.

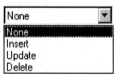

In the **Variables** box, add your variables and give each of them a **Run-time Value**.

Enter your query in the **SQL** pane (or select the fields concerned in the **Database Tables** box and add them to your query using the **COLUMN** button).

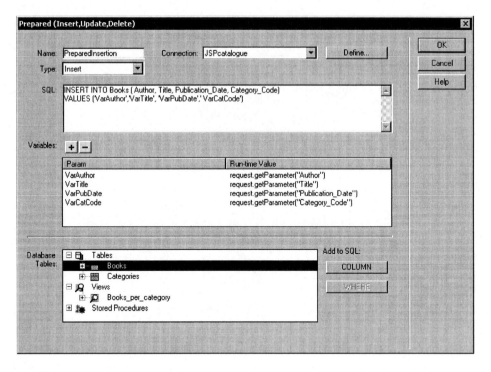

Click **OK**.

Introduction

You can create a dynamic form to display the contents of a record from a database or any other data source. The form objects you can manage include the following:

— text field,

— check box,

— radio button,

— list/menu.

You can insert dynamic text into a page from a data source (such as a database field, a session variable, an application variable or a cookie).

 If you use a dynamic form to consult your database, you must create navigation links to move between records.

The examples set out in this chapter were carried out using an ASP server model.

Creating a dynamic text field

First method

⊟ Select the text field in your form.

⊟ Open the **Data Bindings** window.

⊟ Select a data source.

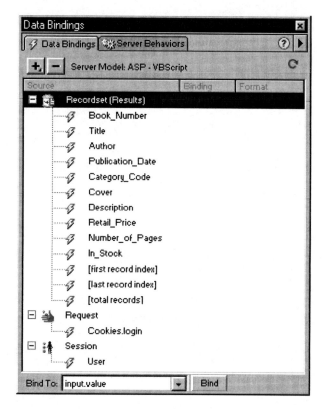

Click the **Bind** button and check that the pop-up menu in the **Binding** column of the **Data Bindings** window is set to **input.value**. Alternatively, you can drag the data source onto the form text field.

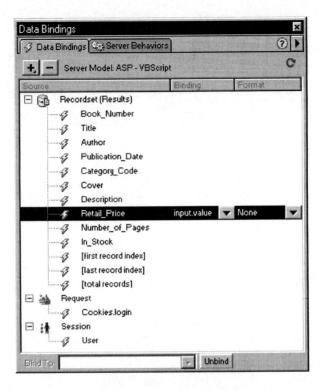

⊡ You can change the presentation format using the pop-up menu in the **Format** column of the **Data Bindings** window.

⊡ To delete the contents of a dynamic field, click the **Unbind** button.

Second method

⊡ Open the **Server Behavior** window, click the 🔲 button and choose **Dynamic Elements - Dynamic Text Field**.

⊡ Select your form field in the **Textfield** pop-up menu.

⊡ Click the 🔲 button, next to the **Set Value To** box and choose your data source.

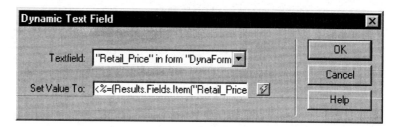

Click **OK**.

If necessary, apply a format using the pop-up menu in the **Format** column of the **Data Binding** window.

Creating a dynamic check box

Select the check box field in your form.

Open the **Server Behavior** window, click the button and choose **Dynamic Elements - Dynamic Check Box**.

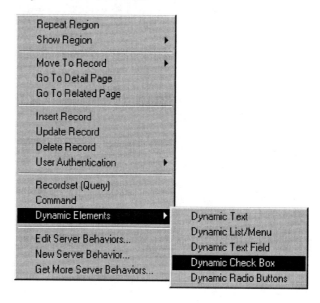

⊡ Select your form field in the **Check Box** pop-up menu.

⊡ Click the 🔲 button, next to the **Check If** box and choose your data source.

⊡ Enter the value that UltraDev must use to determine whether or not it must check the check box.

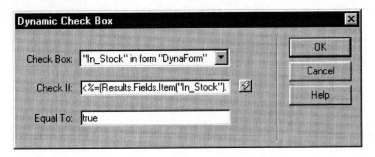

⊡ Click **OK**.

Creating dynamic radio buttons

⊡ Open the **Server Behavior** window, click the 🔲 button and choose **Dynamic Elements - Dynamic Radio Buttons**.

⊡ Select your radio button group in the **Radio Button Group** pop-up menu.

⊡ In the **Value** box, enter a value for each of the buttons in the group (you can also set a button's value in the field's property inspector).

⊡ Click the 🔲 button next to the **Select Value Equal To** box and choose your data source. The value of this data source will determine whether or not the radio button will be activated in the group.

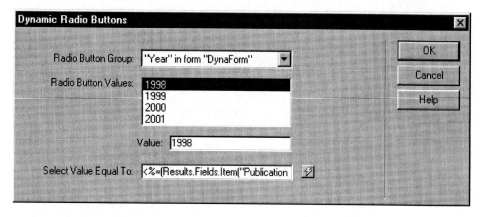

⊟ Click **OK**.

Creating a dynamic list or menu

⊟ Select the **List/menu** field in your form.

⊟ Open the **Server Behavior** window, click the ⊞ button and choose **Dynamic Elements - Dynamic List/Menu**.

⊟ Select a **Recordset** as a data source for your **List/Menu** object.

⊟ Using the **Get Labels From** pop-up menu, choose the database field that contains the labels for your menu.

⊟ Using the **Get Values From** pop-up menu, choose the database field that contains the values for your menu.

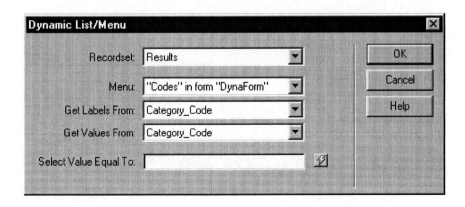

□ The **Select Value Equal To** box is optional. Use this box if you want Ultra-Dev to select an element from your menu by default. In this case, enter a static value or choose a dynamic field using the 🗲 button.

In all cases, the static or dynamic value must correspond to one of your menu element values.

□ Click **OK**.

Inserting dynamic text

*This method is an alternative to that of dragging a dynamic field onto your page from the **Data Bindings** window.*

□ Place the insertion point where you want to insert your dynamic text.

□ Open the **Server Behavior** window, click the ⊞ button and choose **Dynamic Elements - Dynamic Text**.

□ Using the **Field** box, choose your data source (and apply a **Format**, if necessary).

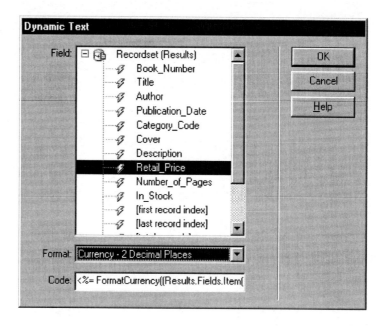

⊡ Click **OK**.

Modifying the properties of a dynamic form field

*You can manage a set of form field properties using the **Data Bindings** window.*

⊡ Select the field in your page.

⊡ Open the **Data Bindings** window.

*By default, the data source is bound to the **input.value** property of the form field.*

⊡ Open the pop-up menu in the **Binding** column to list all the form properties you can associate with a data source.

input.accesskey
input.align
input.alt
input.border
input.checked
input.class
input.disabled
input.height
input.id
input.maxlength
input.name
input.size
input.src
input.style
input.tabindex
input.title
input.type
input.value
input.width

Choose the form property you want to make dynamic.

Introduction

To create dynamic pages, you can bind HTML attributes in your page (such as ActiveX, Flash, Shockwave object parameters or Java applets).

Creating dynamic HTML attributes

Overview

UltraDev marks the HTML properties you can make dynamic with the ⚡ icon.

⊡ Select your HTML object (an image, a table or a layer, for example).

⊡ Choose **Window - Properties** to open the property inspector.

⊡ Click the 🔳 button to display the properties of the selected tag.

⊡ Select the property you want to make dynamic and click the ⚡ icon.

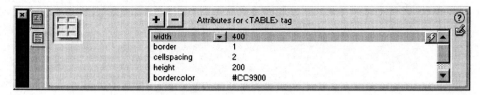

		Attributes for <TABLE> tag	
width	▾	400	
border		1	
cellspacing		2	
height		200	
bordercolor		#CC9900	

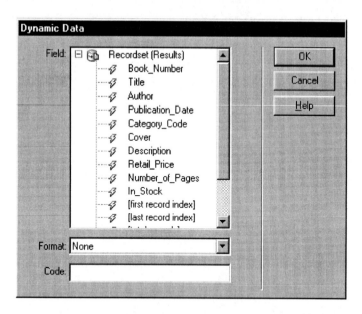

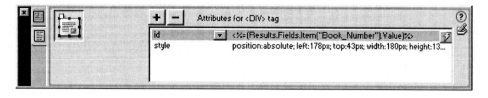

⊡ In the **Field** pane of the **Dynamic Data** dialog box, select the dynamic field you want to bind to this property. If necessary, apply a **Format**.

⊡ Click **OK**.

UltraDev inserts the ASP, JSP or ColdFusion script as a dynamic attribute of the selected HTML tag. For example, for a DIV tag:

Dynamic images

You can insert dynamic images. You can also use a dynamic image as a background image to the page or to a table. The following method applies in all cases, whether you have a dynamic image, a rollover image or a background image.

⊡ To insert a dynamic image:

Insert　　　　　　　　　　　　　　　Ctrl Alt I (PC)
Image　　　　　　　　　　　　　　　　　　　　　　　　⌘ ⌥ I (Mac)

⊡ To insert a background image:

Modify　　　　　　　　　　　　　　　　　　　Ctrl J (PC)
Page Properties　　　　　　　　　　　　　　　⌘ J (Mac)

⊡ To insert a rollover image, navigation bar, Flash button and so forth:

Insert
Interactive Images
Rollover Image or **Navigation Bar** or **Flash Button** etc.

*UltraDev opens a dialog box that allows you to enter your file name or to **Browse** your folders to select your image:*

⊡ In the case of an dynamic image, choose the **Data Sources** option.

⊡ Select the dynamic data source in the **Field** box. If necessary, apply a format using the **Format** pop-up menu.

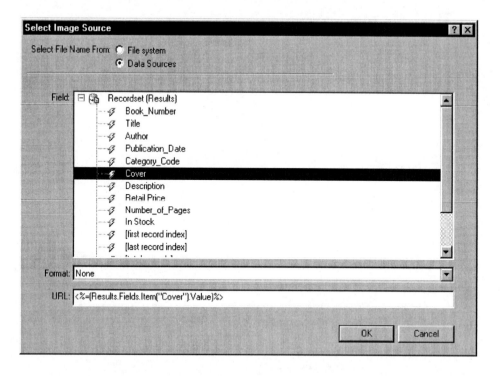

To set the attributes of the dynamic image, select the icon of your dynamic image (▦).

Open the property inspector (**Window - Properties**).

Click the ▣ button to display the properties of the selected tag.

Select the property you want to make dynamic and click the ⚡ icon.

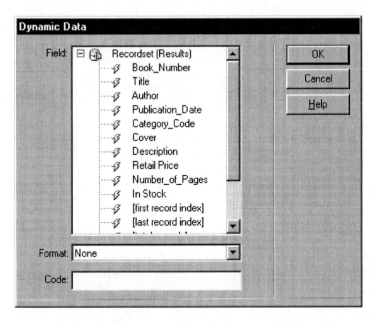

↪ In the **Field** box of the **Dynamic Data** dialog box, select the dynamic field you want to bind to this property. If necessary, apply a **Format**.

↪ Click **OK**.

UltraDev inserts the ASP, JSP or ColdFusion script as a dynamic attribute of the selected HTML tag.

Other image properties

*You can make other image properties dynamic using the **Data Bindings** window.*

↪ Open the **Data Bindings** window and select your image data source.

*By default, the data source is bound to the **img.src** (source file name) property of the dynamic image:*

⊡ Open the pop-up menu in the **Binding** column to list all the image properties you can associate with a data source.

⊡ Choose the image property you want to make dynamic.

Tables

You can make all the properties of a table dynamic (table name, height,
width, frame, colours, background and alignment, for example):

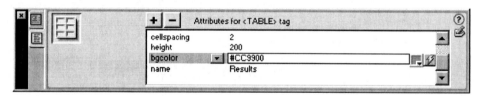

Layers

You can make all the properties of a layer dynamic (the layer **id** and the list of its properties):

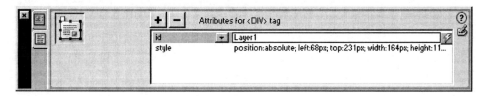

Creating dynamic object parameters

ActiveX, Flash and Shockwave object parameters

The following method applies in all cases, whether you have a Java applet, or a Flash, ActiveX or Shockwave object.

⊡ Select your object.

⊡ Choose **Window - Properties** to open the property inspector.

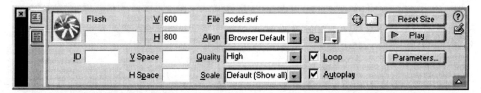

⊡ Click the **Parameters** button.

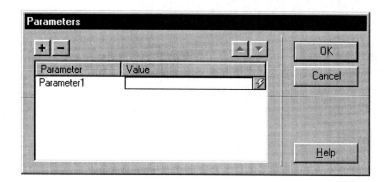

⊡ Enter the name of your parameter and click the 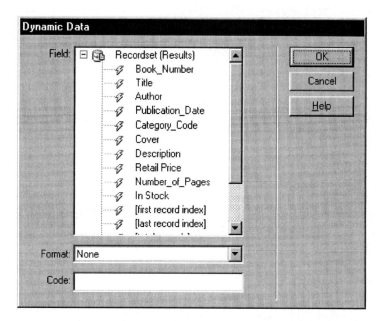 icon in the **Value** column.

In the **Field** box of the **Dynamic Data** dialog box, select the dynamic field you want to bind to this property. If necessary, apply a **Format**.

⊡ Click **OK**.

UltraDev inserts the ASP, JSP or ColdFusion script as a dynamic attribute of the selected HTML tag.

⊟ To set the attributes of your dynamic object, select your Flash, ActiveX, Shockwave or Java applet object, choose **Window - Properties** to open the property inspector then click the 🔲 button to display the properties of the selected tag.

⊟ Select the property you want to make dynamic, click the ⚡ icon and bind an attribute to a data source, as with other objects.

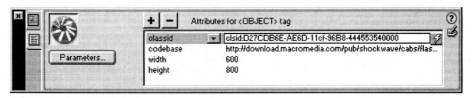

Other object properties

*You can manage a set of object properties using the **Data Bindings** window.*

⊟ Select the object in your page.

⊟ Open the **Data Bindings** window.

*By default, the data source is bound to the **objects.codebase** property of the dynamic object (provided you used the same technique to insert your dynamic object as you would to insert a dynamic image).*

⊟ Open the pop-up menu in the **Binding** column to list all the object properties you can associate with a data source.

```
object.align
object.border
object.class
object.classid
object.codebase
object.codetype
object.data
object.declare
object.height
object.hspace
object.id
object.name
object.shapes
object.standby
object.style
object.title
object.type
object.usemap
object.vspace
object.width
```

Choose the object property you want to make dynamic.

Introduction

A data source is simply an information store that you can use to define the dynamic contents of your Web pages.

You create a data source when you add a recordset. In the **Data Bindings** window, UltraDev lists the dynamic fields you can insert into your page.

In addition to recordsets, you can use other data sources such as session variables, application variables, server variables, JSP JavaBeans and stored procedures. Each server technology has its own peculiarities.

Data sources with ASP

To list the data sources for a page, open the **Data Bindings** window and click the button.

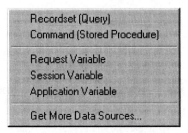

```
Recordset (Query)
Command (Stored Procedure)

Request Variable
Session Variable
Application Variable

Get More Data Sources...
```

Command (Stored Procedure)

*A stored procedure is a set of one or more simple or advanced SQL statements in a database. This set of statements is compiled in the database. This approach enhances the performance of your application. The ASP **Command** object allows you to manage stored procedures. It also allows you to insert, update and delete information in a database.*

Here is an example of a stored procedure on SQL Server:

```
CREATE PROCEDURE CatCode_Procedure
@Category_Code VarChar(3)
AS
SELECT * FROM Books
WHERE Category_Code = @Category_Code
```

-⊟ In the **Data Bindings** window, click the 🔀 button and choose **Command (Stored Procedure)**.

-⊟ Enter a **Name** for your procedure and choose a database **Connection**.

-⊟ From the **Type** pop-up menu, choose **Stored Procedure**, activate the **Return Reordset** check box then enter a name for your recordset in the **Named** box.

-⊟ In the **Database Items** box, select a stored procedure from the **Stored Procedures** branch. Click the **PROCEDURE** button to add your procedure to the **SQL** pane.

-⊟ If your procedure requires parameters, define your variables and all the parameters in the **Variables** box.

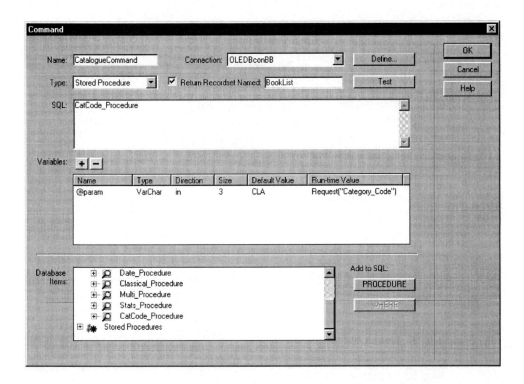

 Microsoft Access considers stored procedures to be SQL views. Consequently, when you use Microsoft Access the **Command** dialog box lists the stored procedures under the **Views** branch in the **Database Items** box. Enter the name of the **View** directly in the **SQL** pane to run your stored procedure via the **Command** object.

Click **OK**.

*Your stored procedure object appears in the **Data Bindings** window as a data source.*

You can include a dynamic data item in your page by selecting it and clicking the **Insert** button or by dragging it onto your page directly.

The **Command** object also allows you to create queries to insert, update or delete data. You can enter your queries or use the graphic editor. UltraDev inserts the default structure of the different types of SQL query:

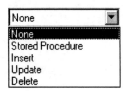

Insert query:

```
INSERT INTO ()
VALUES ()
```

Update query:

```
UPDATE
SET
WHERE
```

Delete query:

```
DELETE FROM
WHERE
```

Request variable

With ASP, a request variable corresponds to using the **Request** object.

⊡ In the **Data Bindings** window, click the ⊞ button and choose **Request Variable**.

⊡ Choose the **Request Variable** you want to add as a data source:

⤶ Enter the **Name** of your variable. Either you must have previously defined your variable or you must use an UltraDev predefined variable. In the case of **ServerVariables** and **ClientCertificates** objects, you must know the syntax of the property you want to use in your ASP documentation.

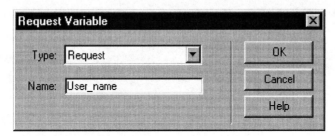

⤶ Click **OK**.

*Your variable appears in the **Data Bindings** window as a data source.*

⤶ You can include your variable in your page by selecting it and clicking the **Insert** button or by dragging it onto your page directly.

 You can use the same technique for all types of request variable. Here is a description of each of the **Request** objects:

Request	provides the contents of a (**POST** or **GET**) form field or a parameter passed in the URL.
Request.Cookie	provides the contents of a cookie.
Request.QueryString	provides the contents of a form field sent with the **GET** method or a parameter passed in the URL: http://www.site.com/filename.asp?variable=value.
Request.Form	provides the contents of a form field sent with the **POST** method.

Request.ServerVariables	provides access to all the server's environment variables: to obtain information concerning the users' browser, enter **HTTP_USER_ AGENT** as the variable **Name**.
Request.ClientCertificates	provides the X.509 standard certification fields of a user query.

Session variable

*With ASP a session variable corresponds to using the **Session** object.*

⤶ In the **Data Bindings** window, click the 🔲 button and choose **Session Variable**.

⤶ Enter the **Name** of your session variable.

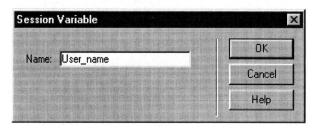

⊡ Click **OK**.

Your variable appears in the **Data Bindings** *window as a data source.*

⊡ You can include your variable in your page by selecting it and clicking the **Insert** button or by dragging it onto your page directly.

 If you choose the **User Authentication - Log In User** server behavior, Ultra-Dev creates two session variables: MM_Username and MM_UserAuthorization.

Application variable

With ASP, an application variable corresponds to using the **Application** *object and the global.asa file.*

⊡ In the **DataBindings** window, click the ⊞ button and choose **Application Variable**.

⊡ Enter the **Name** of your application variable.

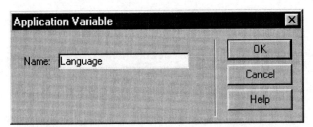

⊡ Click **OK**.

Your variable appears in the **Data Bindings** *window as a data source.*

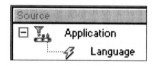

⊡ You can include your variable in your page by selecting it and clicking the **Insert** button or by dragging it onto your page directly.

Data sources with JSP

⊡ To list the data sources for a page, open the **Data Bindings** window and click the ⊞ button.

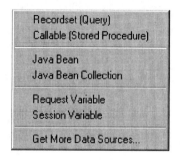

Callable (Stored Procedure)

*A stored procedure is a set of one or more simple or advanced SQL statements in a database. This set of statements is compiled in the database. This approach enhances the performance of your application. The JSP **CallableStatement** object allows you to manage stored procedures. It also allows you to insert, update and delete information in a database.*

Here is an example of a stored procedure on SQL Server:

```
CREATE PROCEDURE CatCode_Procedure
@Category_Code VarChar(3)
AS
SELECT * FROM Books
WHERE Category_Code = @Category_Code
```

⊡ In the **Data Bindings** window, click the 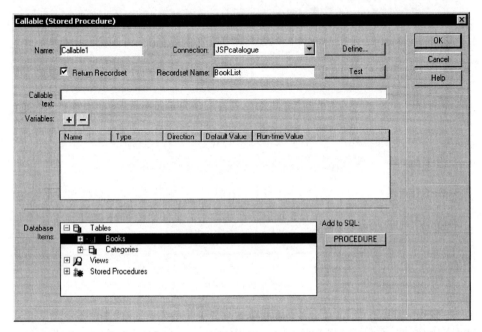 button and choose **Callable (Stored Procedure)**.

⊡ Enter a **Name** for your procedure and choose a database **Connection**.

⊡ Activate the **Return Recordset** check box and enter your **Recordset Name**.

Callable (Stored Procedure)	☒

Name: Callable1   Connection: JSPcatalogue ▼   Define...   OK   Cancel   Help

☑ Return Recordset   Recordset Name: BookList   Test

Callable text: [   ]

Variables: + −

Name	Type	Direction	Default Value	Run-time Value

Database Items:
- ⊟ Tables
  - ⊞ Books
  - ⊞ Categories
- ⊞ Views
- ⊞ Stored Procedures

Add to SQL:
PROCEDURE

⊡ In the **Database Items** box, select a stored procedure from the **Stored Procedures** branch. Click the **PROCEDURE** button to add your procedure to the **Callable text** box.

⊡ If your procedure requires parameters, define your variables and all the parameters in the **Variables** box.

⊡ Click **OK**.

*Your stored procedure object appears in the **Data Bindings** window as a data source.*

⊡ You can include a dynamic data item in your page by selecting it and clicking the **Insert** button or by dragging it onto your page directly.

JavaBean

JavaBeans are software components developed for a specific use. In this case, the JSP page simply calls the JavaBean component, which contains all the instructions the server must run.

 You must copy your (.zip or .jar) class files that contain the beans to the UltraDev folder: Configuration\Classes.

⊡ In the **Data Bindings** window, click the ⊞ button and choose **Java Bean**.

⊡ Enter a **Name** for the bean and choose the **Scope**:

page   to access the object from the page in which you create it.

request   to access the object within the lifespan of the query.

session   to access the object within the lifespan of the session.

application   to access the object within the lifespan of the application.

⊡ Click the **Browse** button to select the classes list for your Java file then choose from the **Class** pop-up menu.

⊡ The property list for your bean appears in the **Properties** box. You can specify a **Default Value** for each of these properties.

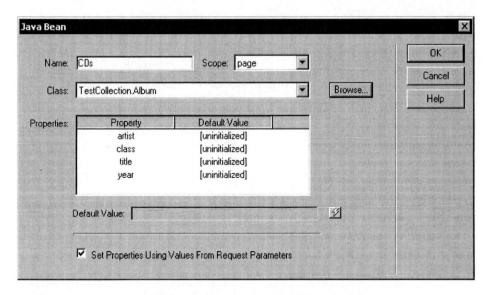

↴ Click **OK**.

*Your **Java Bean** appears in the **Data Bindings** window as a data source.*

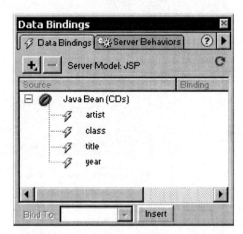

↴ You can include a dynamic data item in your page by selecting it and clicking the **Insert** button or by dragging it onto your page directly.

JavaBean collection

A JavaBean collection is a set of JavaBeans.

- In the **Data Bindings** window, click the button and choose **Java Bean Collection**.

- Click the **Browse** button to select the classes list for your set of Java-Beans then choose from the **Collection Class** pop-up menu.

- Choose the **Indexed Property**, the **Iten Class** and the **Scope**.

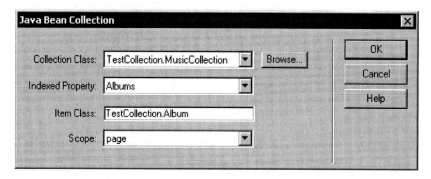

- Click **OK**.

*Your **Java Bean Collection** appears in the **Data Bindings** window as a data source.*

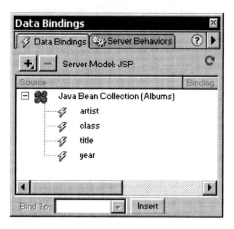

◦ You can include a dynamic data item in your page by selecting it and clicking the **Insert** button or by dragging it onto your page directly.

Request variable

You can extract the contents of a URL value or a form field sent with the POST or GET method.

*With JSP, a request variable corresponds to using the **request.getParameter** object.*

◦ In the **Data Bindings** window, click the 🞥 button and choose **Request Variable**.

◦ Enter the **Name** of your variable.

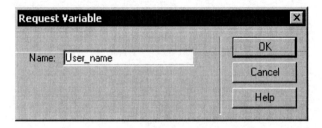

◦ Click **OK**.

*Your variable appears in the **Data Bindings** window as a data source.*

◦ You can include your variable in your page by selecting it and clicking the **Insert** button or by dragging it onto your page directly.

Session variable

*With JSP, a session variable corresponds to using the **Session** object.*

⊡ In the **Data Bindings** window, click the ⊞ button and choose **Session Variable**.

⊡ Enter the **Name** of your variable.

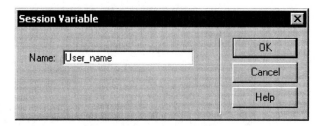

⊡ Click **OK**.

*Your variable appears in the **Data Bindings** window as a data source.*

⊡ You can include your variable in your page by selecting it and clicking the **Insert** button or by dragging it onto your page directly.

Other data sources 2 1 3

Data sources with ColdFusion

⊟ To list the data sources for a page, open the **Data Bindings** window and click the 🔳 button.

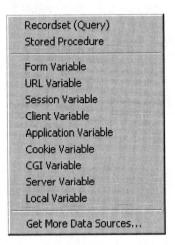

Stored Procedure

*A stored procedure is a set of one or more simple or advanced SQL statements in a database. This set of statements is compiled in the database. This approach enhances the performance of your application. The ColdFusion **<cfstoredproc>** tag allows you to manage stored procedures in a database.*

Here is an example of a stored procedure on SQL Server:

```
CREATE PROCEDURE CatCode_Procedure
@Category_Code VarChar(3)
AS
SELECT * FROM Books
WHERE Category_Code = @Category_Code
```

⊟ In the **Data Bindings** window, click the 🔳 button and choose **Stored Procedure**.

© Editions ENI - All rights reserved

🗂 Enter a **Name** for your procedure and choose a database **Connection**.

🗂 Activate the **Return Recordset** check box and enter your **Recordset Name**.

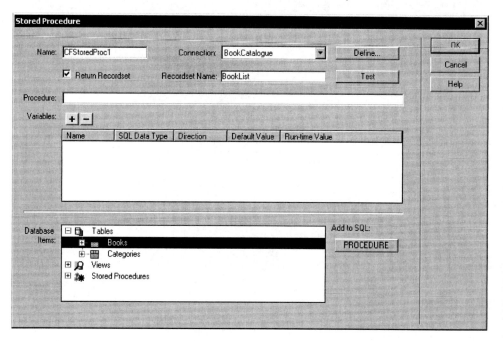

🗂 In the **Database Items** box, select a stored procedure from the **Stored Procedures** branch. Click the **PROCEDURE** button to add your procedure to the **Procedure** box.

🗂 If your procedure requires parameters, define your variables and all the parameters in the **Variables** box.

🗂 Click **OK**.

*Your stored procedure object appears in the **Data Bindings** window as a data source.*

🗂 You can include a dynamic data item in your page by selecting it and clicking the **Insert** button or by dragging it onto your page directly.

Form variable

You can extract the contents of a form field into a form variable.

🗂 In the **Data Bindings** window, click the ⊞ button and choose **Form Variable**.

🗂 Enter the **Name** of your variable.

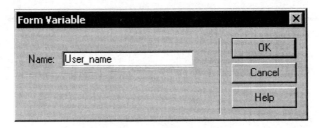

🗂 Click **OK**.

*Your variable appears in the **Data Bindings** window as a data source.*

🗂 You can include your variable in your page by selecting it and clicking the **Insert** button or by dragging it onto your page directly.

URL variable

You can extract the contents of a variable sent via a page's URL.

🗂 In the **Data Bindings** window, click the ⊞ button and choose **URL Variable**.

🗂 Enter the **Name** of your variable.

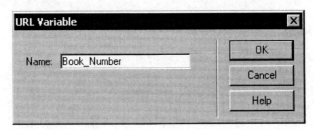

⊡ Click **OK**.

*Your variable appears in the **Data Bindings** window as a data source.*

⊡ You can include your variable in your page by selecting it and clicking the **Insert** button or by dragging it onto your page directly.

Session variable

In a session variable, you can store information concerning a specific user during the whole of the user's visit to your Web site.

⊡ In the **Data Bindings** window, click the 🔘 button and choose **Session Variable**.

⊡ Enter the **Name** of your variable.

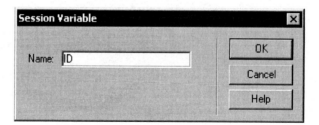

⊡ Click **OK**.

*Your variable appears in the **Data Bindings** window as a data source.*

⊡ You can include your variable in your page by selecting it and clicking the **Insert** button or by dragging it onto your page directly.

Client variable

*As with a cookie variable, in a client variable you can store information concerning a specific user. In addition, the client object contains a number of standard variables. For example, the **Client.LastVisit** variable stores the date of the client's last visit to your site.*

⊡ In the **Data Bindings** window, click the 🔘 button and choose **Client Variable**.

⊟ Enter the **Name** of your variable.

⊟ Click **OK**.

*Your variable appears in the **Data Bindings** window as a data source.*

⊟ You can include your variable in your page by selecting it and clicking the **Insert** button or by dragging it onto your page directly.

Application variable

In an application variable, you can store information at application level. All your site pages can access application variables, irrespective of the client who is using your application.

⊟ In the **Data Bindings** window, click the ⊞ button and choose **Application Variable**.

⊟ Enter the **Name** of your variable.

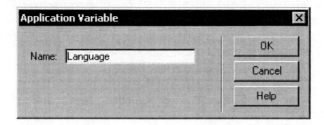

⊟ Click **OK**.

*Your variable appears in the **Data Bindings** window as a data source.*

↴ You can include your variable in your page by selecting it and clicking the **Insert** button or by dragging it onto your page directly.

Cookie variable

↴ In the **Data Bindings** window, click the 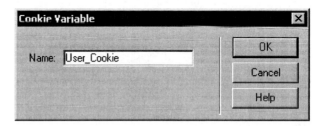 button and choose **Cookie Variable**.

↴ Enter the **Name** of your variable.

Cookie Variable	✕
Name: User_Cookie	OK
	Cancel
	Help

↴ Click **OK**.

*Your variable appears in the **Data Bindings** window as a data source.*

↴ You can include your variable in your page by selecting it and clicking the **Insert** button or by dragging it onto your page directly.

CGI variable

CGI variables are environment variables, such as the IP address (REMOTE_ADDR) or the browser type on a client machine (HTTP_USER_AGENT).

↴ In the **Data Bindings** window, click the 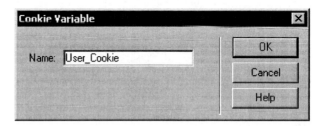 button and choose **CGI Variable**.

↴ Enter the **Name** of your variable.

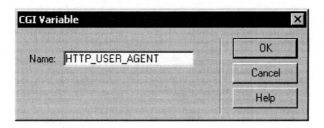

⬆ Click **OK**.

*Your variable appears in the **Data Bindings** window as a data source.*

⬆ You can include your variable in your page by selecting it and clicking the **Insert** button or by dragging it onto your page directly.

Server variable

All users and all applications at server level can access server variables. In addition, ColdFusion provides its own server variables: for example, the Server.OS.Name variable returns the name of the server's operating system.

⬆ In the **Data Bindings** window, click the ➕ button and choose **Server Variable**.

⬆ Enter the **Name** of your variable.

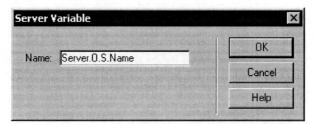

⬆ Click **OK**.

*Your variable appears in the **Data Bindings** window as a data source.*

⬆ You can include your variable in your page by selecting it and clicking the **Insert** button or by dragging it onto your page directly.

Local variable

ColdFusion local variables are created using CFSET or CFPARAM tags, for example: <CFSET variable=value>. You can access local variables at page level.

In the **Data Bindings** window, click the 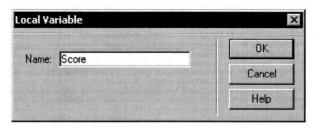 button and choose **Local Variable**.

Enter the **Name** of your variable.

Click **OK**.

*Your variable appears in the **Data Bindings** window as a data source.*

You can include your variable in your page by selecting it and clicking the **Insert** button or by dragging it onto your page directly.

Introduction

You can customise your UltraDev working environment:

— by installing new server behaviors,

— by modifying existing server behaviors,

— by creating your own server behaviors.

Installing new behaviors

You can download new behaviors from the Macromedia Web site then install them using the Macromedia Extension Manager.

In the **Server Behaviors** window, click the button and choose **Get More Server Behaviors** (alternatively, you can use the **Help - Ultradev Exchange** menu option).

This takes you to the Macromedia® site.

Access the Dreamweaver UltraDev part of the site and download the extensions you require.

To download extensions you must be a member of the Macromedia club (you can register on the Macromedia Exchange home page). Next, you must install your extension(s) so that they will appear in the Dreamweaver UltraDev menus.

To install your extensions, choose **Commands - Manage Extensions** (or **Help - Manage Extensions**).

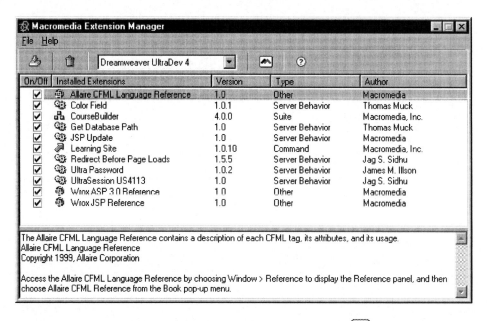

The **Macromedia Extension Manager** window appears. The 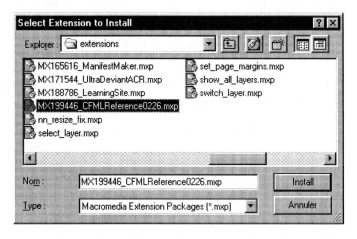 button provides access to the Macromedia Exchange site.

In the **Macromedia Extension Manager** window, choose **File - Install Extension** or click the [ ] button.

Select the extension (an .mxp file) you want to install then click the **Install** button.

*Once the UltraDev has finished installing the extension, the **Macromedia Extension Manager** window shows the name of the extension and a Dreamweaver UltraDev menu offers the corresponding option.*

You can disable an extension by deactivating its check box in the **On/Off** column of the **Macromedia Extension Manager** window.

Modifying existing behaviors

You can adapt UltraDev server behaviors to suit your needs. To modify a behavior, you must first make a copy of it.

 In the **Server Behaviors** window, click the ⊞ button and choose **New Server Behavior**.

 Enter the **Name** of your behavior, activate the **Copy existing server behavior** option and choose from the **Behavior to copy** pop-up menu.

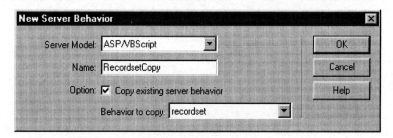

 Click **OK**.

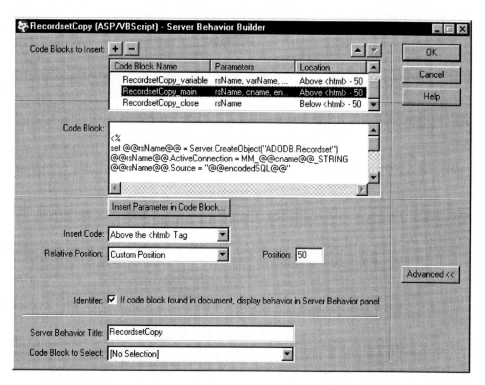

 Choose the **Code Block Name** whose code you want to modify then enter your code in the **Code Block** box.

 Click **OK**.

To modify a custom behavior, click the ![button] button in the **Server Behaviors** window and choose **Edit Server Behaviors**.

If your try to modify an UltraDev component via the **Edit Server Behaviors** dialog box, a message appears advising you to work with a copy of the behavior.

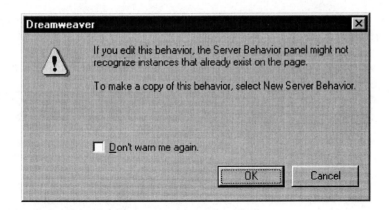

Creating your own behaviors

You can create your own server behaviors. For this purpose, you must enter your own code blocks and indicate where they must act on the html page.

◄┘ In the **Server Behaviors** window, click the ⊞ button and choose **New Server Behavior**.

◄┘ Enter the **Name** of your behavior.

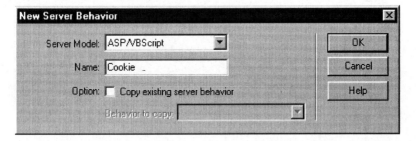

◄┘ Click **OK**.

◄┘ Under **Code Blocks to Insert**, click the ⊞ button to create a new code block. Give your code block a **Name** and click **OK**.

⊡ If you want to insert a parameter in your code block, click the **Insert Parameter in Code Block** button.

⊡ Give the name of the parameter in the **Parameter Name** box.

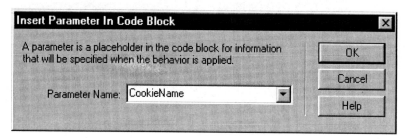

⊡ Click **OK**.

*Your parameter appears in the **Code Block** box in the format @@parameter@@.*

⊡ Using the **Insert Code** pop-up menu, specify where UltraDev must insert the code in the page.

⊡ Using the **Relative Position** pop-up menu, specify how UltraDev must insert the code blocks: either with respect to the tags on the page or with respect to the selected tag. The **Custom Position** option allows you to define the order in which UltraDev must position the code blocks. For this purpose you must enter a value between 0 and 99 in the **Position** box.

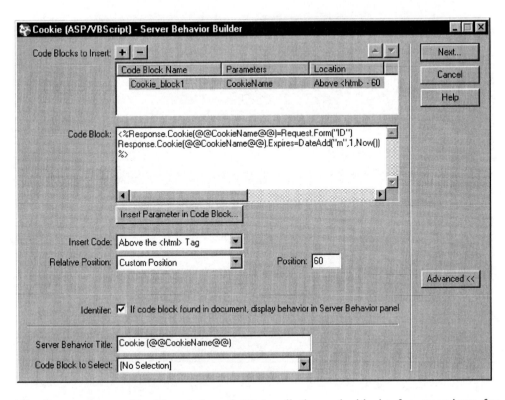

*UltraDev assigns a **Position** value of 50 to all the code blocks for recordsets for insertion **Above the html Tag**.*

Click the **Next** button and modify the value in the **Display As** column as required (for example, you could associate your parameter with a dynamic text field).

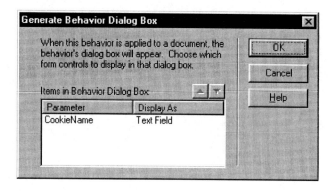

Click **OK**.

Once UltraDev has created your behavior, it includes it in the list of **Server Behaviors** *and allows you to use it.*

In the **Server Behaviors** window, click the button and choose your new behavior.

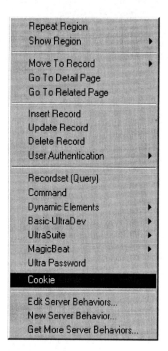

If you defined any parameters for your behavior, enter their values in the dialog box that appears.

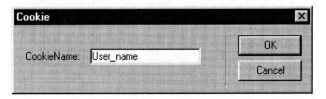

UltraDev inserts the code blocks in your html page at the positions you indicated in the **Insert Code** and **Relative Position** pop-up menus.

```
<%LANGUAGE="VBSCRIPT"%>
<%Response.Cookie(User_name)=Request.Form("ID")
Response.Cookie(User_name).Expires=DateAdd("m",1,Now())
%>
<html>
```

You can **Edit** or **Remove** your server behavior after selecting it in the **Edit Server Behaviors** dialog box, which you can access from the **Server Behaviors** window.

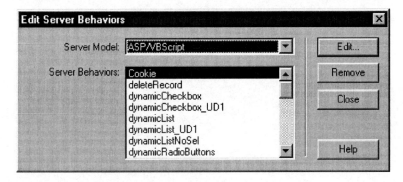

UltraDev server behaviors

Behaviors common to ASP, JSP and ColdFusion

You can apply these behaviors with ASP, JSP or ColdFusion.

Repeat Region	allows you to display all your recordset data on one page.
Show Region	allows you to display or mask specific regions in your results page.
Move To Record	allows you to create navigation objects.
Go To Detail Page	allows you to create a link between a master page and a detail page.
Go To Related Page	allows you to link two pages and pass form or URL parameters between them.
Insert Record	allows you to insert a new record in the database.
Update Record	allows you to update a record in the database.
Delete Record	allows you to delete a record from the database.
User Authentication	allows you to create a set of pages for managing site access.
Recordset (Query)	allows you to create a data table to receive the results of an SQL query on a database.
Dynamic Elements	allows you to create dynamic text and form objects.

Behaviors specific to ASP

Command	allows you to run stored procedures in a database (in addition to data insert, update and delete queries).

Behaviors specific to JSP

Java Bean   allows you to run JavaBeans.

Java Bean Collection   allows you to use a set of JavaBeans.

**Prepared
(Insert, Update, Delete)** allows you to create precompiled insert, update and delete queries.

**Callable
(Stored Procedure)**   allows you to run stored procedures in a database.

Behaviors specific to ColdFusion

Stored Procedure   allows you to run stored procedures in a database.

UltraDev live objects

Master Detail Page Set creates a master page and a detail page allowing you to pass URL parameters between them.

**Recordset
Navigation Bar**   creates text or image recordset navigation links.

**Recordset
Navigation Status**   creates a recordset counter.

Record Insertion Form   creates a record insertion form along with the required server behaviors.

Record Update Form   creates a record update form along with the required server behaviors.

ADO   ActiveX Data Object: an ASP object that allows you to access databases via ODBC or OLEDB.

Application server Server software that runs ASP, JSP or Cold-Fusion scripts.

ASP   Active Server Pages: Microsoft® technology for creating dynamic Web pages.

CFML   ColdFusion Markup Language: a ColdFusion specific tag based markup language

ColdFusion   Allaire Corporation proprietary technology for creating dynamic Web pages.

DSN   Data Source Name: an ODBC data source

HTTP   HyperText Transfer Protocol: the protocol that underlies the World Wide Web.

Java   a high-level programming language used with JSP.

JDBC   Java DataBase Connectivity: a protocol for connecting databases with JSP.

JScript   Microsoft Javascript: a scripting language used with ASP (see also VBscript).

JSP   Java Server Pages: Sun Microsystems technology for creating dynamic Web pages.

MDAC   Microsoft Data Access Components: Microsoft components that include ODBC and OLE DB drivers for accessing databases.

ODBC   Open DataBase Connectivity: a protocol that allows you to connect to most commercially available databases (see also DSN).

OLEDB   a Microsoft component that provides standardised access to all data sources including databases.

Primary key   a unique identifier in a database.

Query	a request to extract, update or modify information in a database.
RDBMS	Relational DataBase Management System.
Recordset	a set of data records you can use with ASP and ColdFusion (see also Resultset).
Resultset	a set of data records you can use with JSP (see also Recordset).
Server behavior	a set of server-side scripts that allow you to implement dynamic Web pages.
Server-side scripts	a set of procedures that the application server runs.
SQL	Structured Query Language: a language for handling database information.
URL	Uniform Resource Locator: the address of a Web page.
VBscript	Visual Basic script: a scripting language used with ASP (see also JScript).

A

ACCESS RIGHTS

See ACCESSING SITES

ACCESSING SITES

ACTIVEX

APPLICATION SERVER

ASP

See also APPLICATION SERVER, CONNECTIONS

B

BEHAVIORS

C

COLDFUSION

See also APPLICATION SERVER, CONNECTIONS

CONNECTIONS

List of available titles
in the Studio Factory collection

Visit our Internet site for the list of the latest titles published.
http://www.eni-publishing.com

Dreamweaver 3

Dreamweaver 4

Dreamweaver Ultradev 4

Flash 5